VOICE
MATTERS:
AN ANTHOLOGY OF
PUBLIC RELATIONS
WITH A CONSCIENCE

ISBN: 1463753667
ISBN 13: 9781463753665

Library of Congress Control Number: 2011913249
CreateSpace, North Charleston, SC

Cover Design by Richard Montgomery

Contents

The Ear is An Organ
Made for Love

E. ETHELBERT MILLER

(for Me-K)

It was the language that left us first.
The Great Migration of words. When people
spoke they punched each other in the mouth.
There was no vocabulary for love. Women
became masculine and could no longer give
birth to warmth or a simple caress with their
lips. Tongues were overweight from profanity
and the taste of nastiness. It settled over cities
like fog smothering everything in sight. My
ears begged for camouflage and the chance
to go to war. Everywhere was the decay of
how we sound. Someone said it reminded
them of the time Sonny Rollins disappeared.
People spread stories of how the air would
never be the same or forgive. It was the end
of civilization and nowhere could one hear
the first notes of *A Love Supreme*. It was as
if John Coltrane had never been born.

Foreword

BOB HERBERT

America is losing its way. While lavishing trillions on wars in the Middle East, we're wielding the budget ax on schools and libraries and laying off teachers, police officers, firefighters and other essential public employees. Our nation's once-powerful middle class has become a vast army of displaced workers unable to find or keep the full-time employment necessary to provide security for their families and set in motion a brighter future for their children. We have undergone a massive and wholly perverse redistribution of wealth from the bottom up, from the poor and the middle classes to those who were already extremely well-off.

Dizzying changes (and not for the better) are occurring in the country that led the way in the establishment of a vast and upwardly mobile middle class. Income inequality in the United States has reached extremes not seen since the days leading up to the Great Depression, and there is no reversal in sight. Recent data has shown that the richest 5 percent of the population has amassed 63.5 percent of the nation's wealth. The vast majority, the bottom 80 percent, holds a mere 12.8 percent of the wealth. Incredibly, the richest 10 percent of Americans garnered 100 percent of the average income growth from 2000 to 2007. No good can come of such gross inequality. This unconscionable imbalance is already undermining our democracy and hampering efforts to bring about a robust economic recovery.

The American dream is on life support in this demoralizing environment in which all power is being shifted to those who are already at or near the top

Simply stated, the economy is a disaster for huge swaths of the population. At last count, more than 25 million Americans were unemployed or working part-time because they could not find full-time work. Six million manufacturing jobs disappeared from the economy in the last decade of 2000 to 2010. Two million construction jobs vanished when the housing market crashed in the Great Recession. Many of those jobs will never return. Millions of college graduates are working at jobs that do not require a college degree, putting downward pressure on men and women with just a high-school education or less. Those less well-educated workers are being forced into even more menial work—or out of the labor market entirely.

There is, frankly, a war against working people and the poor in this country. While scores of millions of families are reeling from the effects of sustained economic hardship, increasing numbers of elected officials are bowing to the interests of the corporate classes and have chosen this precise moment to further rend the already-tattered social safety net. They are not moved by the suffering and anguish of so many struggling Americans. Wages and benefits for public workers are under furious assault, and, in many parts of the country, the fundamental right of workers to organize on behalf of their own interests is being curtailed.

The American dream is on life support in this demoralizing environment in which all power is being shifted to those who are already at or near the top. Young people find themselves confronting a future in which they will likely be less well-off than their parents. Opportunities are shrinking—rather than *expanding*—in this new American reality. While the corporate elite thrive as never before, such crucial components of American life as Medicare, Social

Security, public education and government support for homeowners and the unemployed are being attacked as unaffordable and inessential, even as we allocate trillions earmarked for war.

The consequences are both painful and extreme. Nearly 45 million Americans are poor. One in every five American children and more than a third of all Black children are poor. Public schools in many parts of the country are in a wretched state, as is the nation's infrastructure. Many urban centers have been driven to their knees economically. The number of African American men in prison now exceeds the number enslaved at the start of the Civil War. Our "more perfect union" has foundered on the shores of greed, selfishness, ignorance and self-destruction.

The good news in this harrowing scenario is that there are still brave and effective souls resisting the terrible tide. Too rarely do we hear about those who are fighting back—people like Susan Burton, a formerly incarcerated African American woman who welcomes newly released female prisoners as they are dropped off (the word "dumped" comes to mind) at a bus station near skid row in downtown Los Angeles and offers these women the crucial help they need to begin rebuilding their lives; people like Larry Adelman, who knows that zip codes are more important than genetic codes in determining the quality of people's lives and how long they are likely to survive and has transformed that understanding into a remarkable film series on health equity; people like Diann Rust-Tierney, who travels tirelessly to America's death rows, rallying support to end the scourge of capital punishment; and people like Metropolitan Washington transit union leader Jackie Jeter who, often in the face of official opprobrium, fights tenaciously for safe conditions for her workers and all riders of public transit.

It is often hard, amid the din, to hear the voices of these courageous individuals; and that is where the wonderful and formidable Gwen McKinney enters the picture. Her belief in these individuals, in their vision and determination and in their ability to spark the kind of crucial changes this country so desperately needs is at the core of the work of McKinney & Associates. With skill and creativity, and with passion and great devotion, she finds ways for these voices to be heard. After two decades in the trenches, McKinney and her colleagues know that change does not happen quickly or predictably. But they carry on with the confidence that change for the better can come, as long as those voices continue to rise above the chaos, their words and their examples inspiring us like glints of light in a deep, dark tunnel.

We need those voices now more than ever. Overwhelming imbalances in wealth and income inevitably result in enormous imbalances of political power, so the corporations and the very wealthy continue to do well, the employment crisis never gets addressed, the wars never end and nation-building never gets a foothold here at home. New ideas, strong voices and inspired leadership have seldom been more urgently needed. There is a fierce hunger in the land for those who call for peace, who fight without respite on behalf of schools and children and access to quality health care, who stand up boldly for the rights of workers and trade unions and who give no quarter in the continuing campaign for racial justice. This book could not have come at a more crucial moment. Let us heed these vibrant voices that still believe in—and act for—America's promises.

Introduction

DIANE MCKINNEY-WHETSTONE

A tragedy sideswiped Gwen McKinney shortly after her relocation to Washington DC. It was 1982, and she'd arrived in the nation's capital, bursting with the exuberance and tenacity of a West Philly girl nurtured by a politician father and a loving and fiercely outspoken mother. Her skills had been sharpened by close siblings—five sisters and a brother—doling out healthy blends of criticism, competition and adoration.

She'd left behind a successful journalism career at the *Philadelphia Tribune,* the nation's oldest Black newspaper. Though she was only 27, she'd already co-founded the National Alliance of Third World Journalists the year before. The decade of the 1980s would take her and the NATWJ on fact-finding missions across the world, from Lebanon to Grenada to several stints to Angola, Zimbabwe, Cuba and the former Warsaw Pact countries of Czechoslovakia, East Germany and the Soviet Union. It was late September, just two weeks after her arrival in DC, and she was rushing across a busy intersection, in pursuit of a deadline, to catch the bus. Before she even heard the first screech of tires or felt the initial impact of the car's bumper, she was propelled upward through the air. She describes that moment as having the sense of hands rushing under her to scatter the pull of gravity then turning her over and over again, as if positioning her so that she would fall where the impact would do least harm.

There was no lasting harm, even though the DC police presented her with a memorable token in the hospital emergency room: a jaywalking ticket. But there was, in that near-catastrophe, the refinement of a guiding principle: ultimately, unseen hands will rush in to buffet, supplant and even reposition so that she is situated where the potential for a good outcome is maximized. She knew then that she could take calculated risks and that her determined spirit would guide her. Her unique public-relations agency was soon to be born.

Academicians generally agree that successful business owners share some common characteristics: a passion for the core mission of the company; the ability to inspire, to collaborate; a natural curiosity; a nonconformist's bent; vision for both the long and short term and a ferociously competitive spirit.

That determined spirit had already served Gwen McKinney well, as the middle child who had learned how to throw elbows to get attention. It propelled her academically as she battled an undiagnosed, mild form of dyslexia and, essentially, taught herself to read the way she needed to learn to read. Indeed, that determined spirit was at work in October of 1990, when Gwen and her friend and journalism colleague Leila McDowell hung a "Women at Work" shingle on the basement office in the St. Augustine Church Ecumenical Center. That 12' by 12' space served as the incubator for the thriving public-relations firm to come.

The personality of a company often mimics the personality of its founder. That McKinney churned its way from that church basement to its current prestigious location at 16th and K Streets in Northwest DC would not surprise Gwen McKinney's clients and associates. District delegate Eleanor Holmes Norton, the firm's first official client, would not be surprised. Nor would South African then-president Nelson Mandela; the courageous anti-apartheid leader had engaged the new firm of McKinney & MacDowell to manage his media relations during his second visit to the United States. Certainly, Elaine Jones would have predicted the company's success. As president of the NAACP Legal Defense Fund, Jones selected the agency to represent the nation's preeminent civil rights law firm. Says Jones, "We knew the law, but we didn't know how to talk about the law in ways that could show people how legal opinion affects their daily lives. Gwen taught us how to do that."

Kemba Smith is grateful that she did.

As a college student, Kemba became romantically involved with a notorious drug dealer; she even dropped out of school to be with him, traveling the country while he committed heinous criminal acts that included drug trafficking and murder. When Kemba returned home, she turned herself in. She quickly realized that she'd have to reveal her boyfriend's whereabouts to purchase her own freedom. It was too late. He had been murdered in Seattle. The government would make its case against Kemba instead. In 1994, Kemba Smith was charged with conspiracy to distribute crack cocaine, money laundering and making false statements. She was sentenced to 24.5 years as a result of amendments to the Anti-Drug Abuse Act of 1986 that allowed prosecutors to convict people based merely on the assumption that they *should* have known about criminal activity.

Elaine Jones and her team with the NAACP Legal Defense Fund (LDF) mounted a rousing challenge on Kemba's behalf; but there would need to be more—*much* more—as the case wound its way through the criminal-justice system and the court of public opinion. It is a paradox in the transmission of information that facts do not always equal the truth. Charged with leading the LDF's public-relations efforts, Gwen McKinney was acutely aware that the mere recitation of facts in the Kemba Smith case would more veil than reveal the truth. The facts would need to be arranged so that Kemba's true story would emerge.

Kemba Smith was the good-girl daughter of professional parents living in a predominately white suburb of Richmond, Virginia. She'd had a sheltered upbringing, not even being allowed to date until her senior year in high school. She left home in 1989 to attend Hampton University. Her social awkwardness was so painful during her first semester that she did what she thought she must do in order to fit in. As a result, she fell in with the wrong crowd, becoming infatuated with a dashing devil in the form of Peter Hall, aka Khalif—a nonstudent hanger-around-campus. He was charming at first, seductive; she felt comfortable with him, protected. By the time his masks came off, she was already ensnared. He inflicted physical and psychological abuse, even threatening to harm her family. The threat of his violent nature rang true. He reportedly murdered one of his own friends.

Working closely with the public-relations-savvy Elaine Jones, Gwen knew Kemba's story had resonance. That Kemba ran away with Hall is a script that gets acted out time and again in the lives of women who've been abused. Gwen allowed that fact to have its just prominence as she arranged the story's messages so that the facts would illuminate the truth. But there was something else going on; it had to do with Kemba's upbringing. That sheltered, middle-class, adored-daughter upbringing was familiar to Gwen because it mirrored the upbringing of the daughters of her closest friends—even her own niece. It became a pitch point in the story. Kemba's crime was one of poor judgment at a time in a young woman's life when she is the most fragile: when she leaves, for the first time, a nurturing family that has given her everything she needs save street smarts. Hall had pounced on that fragility, to Kemba's devastation.

With Elaine as key strategist and public voice, Gwen helped explain Kemba's story in a way that engaged parents everywhere; she appealed not just to the intellect but to the conscience—to the sense of right and wrong. The "with a conscience identifier" at the end of the firm's name became a beating heart. Public sentiment in support of Kemba rode a wave all the way to the White House. On December 22, 2000, in his final hours as president, Bill Clinton issued a presidential clemency freeing Kemba Smith; she'd served six years. Working closely with LDF, McKinney's brand of public relations with a conscience had succeeded in the most significant way.

McKinney has excelled in replicating the traditional media relations practice of public relations. The firm's clients have appeared on far-reaching media—from ABC's *Nightline* to NBC's *Today* from NPR and MSNBC to CNN. They have been profiled and quoted in the *New York Times, the Washington Post, Newsweek, Essence, Ebony, Glamour* and *Jet* and in targeted media—from community papers to urban radio and to trade and professional journals. Today, clients benefit from the firm's adeptness at utilizing new media and technologies in all of their emerging forms..

The firm has also synthesized an array of services that foster a unified, coherent and power-packed campaign. Clients come to McKinney & Associates knowing that they want to get their message out but not knowing how to do it. McKinney works closely with them to hone their message and then writes speeches, plans speaking tours, arranges panels, conducts conferences, orchestrates special events and media trains an organization's spokespeople so that they shine when they are in the spotlight.

But McKinney really distinguishes itself in the practice of public relations by insisting that the firm's work pulses with a sense of conscience. McKinney is very selective with its client roster. It is no coincidence that a McKinney client will not only embody a determined spirit—much like the drive and determination that is a hallmark of Gwen's own makeup—but that clients will most assuredly be involved in work that advances social justice. From assuring full voting rights to those displaced by Hurricane Katrina to mitigating the inequities in health care for Black women and infants, the core missions of McKinney's clients revolve around issues that engage Gwen's passion. As a result, her work on their behalf is as dazzling as it is tenacious.

On June 22, 2009, a Metro train was stopped on the rails north of the Fort Totten Station in Northeast Washington. It was the height of rush hour. A train operated by 42-year-old Jeanice McMillan barreled into the rear of the stalled train. McMillan and eight others were killed. Early news reports hinted at operator error as the reason for the crash. At the time, McKinney represented the Amalgamated Transit Union Local 689 whose workers, like Jeanice McMillan, operate the Metro. The firm was quick to gather all the facts relating to the tragedy—and the facts showed quite the opposite. Automatic train-control systems had failed, and McMillan had used the full weight of her body to manually apply brakes. Though sheer physics prevented her from stopping the many tons of steel, she was able to slow the train to a point where impact was lessened, likely saving hundreds of lives. McKinney, working closely with the transit union leadership, ensured that that truth was brought to light. By the time of her funeral, McMillan had been rightfully cast as a hero.

In McKinney's brand of public relations, we see the determined spirit that has grown a company from a closet-sized basement office to a gracious suite at 16th and K.

After two decades, the firm has no dearth of organizations and issues that clamor for its specialized, sensitive and conscientious treatment. Today, health policy looms large on our national agenda, and McKinney is working with the Robert Wood Johnson Foundation to provide strategic support to grantees of the nation's largest health philanthropy. Issues of Black women's health tug especially deep for Gwen, whose own mother died at a young 56 years old. McKinney conducted a multifaceted campaign, *BeWellWomen*, sponsored by the University of California, San Francisco, and the California Department of Public Health. Centered on preconception health, it is a typical McKinney focus of energy, one where the facts—that Black women are more likely to be obese, die younger and have smaller birth weight children—needed to get their just arrangement so that the truth of the story could shine through. That truth looks beyond one's penchant for a Big Mac vs. a salad and addresses the tough, underlying questions about how a woman's sense of worth affects her health and how the disparities she suffers daily determine her sense of worth.

Architects speak of "form following function" when a structure's design matches its intended use. Students of literature reference form to content when the style of a story's rendering mimics the story being told. Those same principles are at work here. Whether it was publicizing the 2003 Stanley Nelson film, *The Murder of Emmet Till*, planning for the media and publicity surrounding the 50th anniversary of *Brown v. Board of Education* or current work to empower young Black women to protect the health of their families, in McKinney's brand of public relations we see the determined spirit that has grown a company from a closet-sized basement office to a gracious suite at 16th and K.

That same determination drives the company's founder, who acknowledges the presence of unseen hands that have buffered, supplanted and repositioned her throughout her life. In a seamless expression of form to content, McKinney & Associates has itself become those hands, engaging the public, uncloaking and clarifying the message and ensuring that the facts are rightly positioned, the truth is luminous and conscience is resonant throughout.

A Way Out of No Way: From Challenge to Cause to Crusade

LEILA MCDOWELL

The theme song of black America could be titled "make a way out of no way." We have turned the slave masters' throwaway greens and discarded pig guts into culinary delicacies. We have fought the unbending power of entrenched segregation and slavery. Through our struggle, we have advanced democracy for all Americans and sparked movements for progressive social change. We are the culture that fuels the American character. The creativity, resourcefulness and determination of African American people have produced the most transformative social change in the United States, created a model for other social-justice movements and served as a seminal catalyst for a metamorphosis that reverberated around the world. And while few of us will ever face the daunting challenges of our ancestors, their theme song should be our guiding force.

Making a way out of no way often framed my own advocacy for Layla, my daughter who suffers from severe autism, seizure disorder and other intellectual disabilities. When she was in middle school, she became aggressive in her method of communicating with others. Dr. Martin Luther King, Jr., once said that "a riot is the voice of the unheard." My daughter's quiet riots emerged from being locked in the prison of autism, unable to communicate her frustration or anxiety. Aggression is not uncommon for people with autism. It is best addressed with a well-developed behavior plan that teaches alternative ways to end the silence within which many with autism are held captive.

Layla's frustration and anger found expression in her violence. The best way for my daughter to learn how to interact with "normal" folks was to *be around* them. If you want to learn French, the most effective method is to immerse yourself in a French-speaking environment. If we want people with autism or intellectual disabilities to be an integral part of society and learn social norms, we need them to be immersed in society.

We also discovered that one of Layla's teachers would pinch her neck when she didn't do what the teacher wanted and that my daughter was far too often warehoused without a lot to do in her classroom. Fairfax County schools had a formula for children like her. It was simple: send them away to a self-contained, institutionalized setting where, if they acted with aggression, they would be held in isolation for hours at a time in barren rooms often no bigger than a closet. This would be awful for any of us; for someone with autism it is a nightmare. Because she would be in an institutionalized setting with many nonverbal peers, our ability to know what was really happening would be impossible. Whether she was abused, ignored or warehoused—even with surprise visits from us (which they discouraged and blocked)—we would likely not know what went on there. In her mainstream public school, it was through a non-autistic peer in the general classroom that we learned about the teacher's aide with a fondness for pinching special education students. Fairfax County, an affluent school district, had another trick up its sleeve for parents of children with disabilities who dared to buck the system: a bevy of well-paid attorneys who were on retainer for millions of dollars. Fairfax County was accustomed to wealthy parents attempting to advocate for their children by hiring lawyers, so the county perfected legal strategies to successfully beat back even the best cases. Most parents, after spending tons of money—some almost toward bankruptcy—still failed in court. For us, retaining a high-priced attorney was not even an option. We could no more afford an expensive attorney to fight Fairfax County than we could buy a yacht to travel around the world or feast on a daily meal of caviar.

The prospects for keeping my daughter in her public school were bleak, to say the least, so I drew on my people's heritage and began to plot a strategy. We knew that a legal plan alone was not going to win this battle, but we were fortunate to find, through a fellow parent, a tax attorney who volunteered to at least put on a show for us and help us initially with the case. She didn't really know special-education law and wasn't going to take this all the way to court, but she was an imposing figure: a tough, aggressive, IRS-fighting lady. This formidable woman came into our first few meetings with the top education officials with sufficient bravado, saying, "I'm locked and loaded and ready to go." Little did they know that she had no plans to come back. But smoke and mirrors and a little bluster are not bad things.

I then called on my background as an activist and contacted disability-rights organizations around the area to stage a demonstration in front of my daughter's school. My son recruited some of his friends, so we had an effective multigenerational visual. We all held up colorful, handwritten signs around the theme of "integration not segregation." Crafting an effective message was key. It was simple and easily understood and played into a value-and-information frame that most people already embraced. We didn't want the message to be diverted into a special-education debate; rather, we wanted it to revolve around the civil-rights issue of integration.

Ours was the first demonstration in the history of Herndon Middle School. The frantic reaction from the principal and staff to scores of people, press and police converging on the school was reminiscent of the Keystone Kops running into each other trying to contain the chaos. We knew that media attention was essential; we had to embarrass the school system and win in the "court of public opinion" if we were ever going to have a chance.

One of the parents supporting us was from the military (just for the record, I am deeply opposed to our cruel military adventures in Iraq, Libya and Afghanistan). She counseled that we needed to use a "shock and awe" strategy rather than a gentle escalating strategy of pressure. She said that I had to unleash everything I had, because they wouldn't know if there was more coming, and that was the only way I could intimidate a foe as powerful and skilled as Fairfax County. And she was right; at that moment, I could not see any other cards that we could play, so I had to roll out big. (I tend to advocate that maxim now to many of my clients: roll out big, create an attention-getting debut of a campaign so that everything else that follows generates notice.)

So I put on my PR hat, crafted a good story, added the graphic of a little girl being locked out of a classroom and started pitching and pitching and pitching. Our story became an ongoing news story—we were followed by local news cameras and print reporters every step of the way. When our conflict escalated to a tense meeting with the superintendent of schools, the cameras came with me. I contacted all my friends with any organization that had a name and asked them to send letters to the county about concern over segregation. Their support was invaluable and generated more media coverage. I will always be grateful to my client Alan Curtis, president and CEO of the Eisenhower Foundation, who not only wrote a letter but came to stand with me at the demonstration.

> *I earned the nickname 'Mom from Hell.' But I wore that name like a badge of honor.*

Fairfax County does not like airing its dirty laundry, and it does not like being embarrassed. It finally relented and allowed my daughter Layla to go to her public high school. Apparently, I earned the nickname "Mom from Hell." But I wore that name like a badge of honor. The district provided the necessary support—a special aide and an autism specialist with a well-thought-out behavior plan—so that Layla could learn alternative strategies for communication. They stimulated her with interesting activities and learning opportunities. The aides and specialists worked gently and carefully to move her from aggression to communication. She demonstrated to all that with the right support, any child can do well. The program at her high school became a model for students like her—keeping them in society and not isolating them in the darkness of segregation.

Parents became inspired by the victory, and we formed an organization called Neighborhood Schools Now, which advocates for children with disabilities to be integrated into their neighborhood schools. Formerly, many kids were bussed hours away to go to segregated classrooms. Federal law—the Individuals with Disabilities Education Act —says that children with disabilities have a right to be educated in the "least restrictive setting," but many school systems find loopholes in that right. Today, Layla is thriving and doing community service at the library and with senior-citizen centers, Meals on Wheels and food banks. She is an integral part of society, happy and able to communicate. She has not been aggressive in more than 12 years. And Fairfax County implemented several full-integration initiatives that endure today. As with any victory, we will have to always struggle to protect our achievement, but the story offers a lesson for winning.

My experience fighting for my daughter's education echoed so much of the work that Gwen McKinney and I undertook at McKinney & McDowell. Many times we faced trying to generate attention for stories that did not easily lend themselves to coverage. My daughter's case was one of those—a story that had to be "mined" to surface a salient point, an interesting parallel; segregation was the gold I discovered. Generating a spotlight, framing or reframing the message, being aggressive and not taking no for an answer are all principles that allow us to "make a way out of no way" and effectively use strategic communications to help achieve a victory. One memorable effort was the case of Lacresha Murray, who was serving a 25-year prison term after being found guilty of beating a two-and-a-half-year-old girl to death. The killing occurred in Austin in 1996, when Lacresha was 11.

In the second installment of a series on the case, entitled "In America; How Did Jayla Die?" the great former *New York Times* columnist Bob Herbert wrote:

> Dr. [Linda] Norton is a former Dallas County Medical Examiner who is now in private practice. She is recognized as an expert in matters of child abuse and neglect and has testified frequently for the prosecution in child-abuse cases.
>
> This time, for the first time, she testified for the defense.
>
> "I have been doing forensic pathology since 1974," she said in an interview, "and I have never had a case affect me like this one. Lacresha Murray is an innocent child."
>
> Lacresha, who has learning difficulties and is big for her age (which played into the prosecution's efforts to portray her as an 11-year-old monster), was convicted of criminally negligent homicide and injury to a child in the death of Jayla Belton. Lacresha was said to have attacked Jayla with such force that she broke four ribs and ruptured her liver.

> There was no legitimate evidence against her, just a "confession" that even prosecutors have acknowledged would not have accounted for the injuries that killed Jayla. There were no witnesses and no murder weapon, and police investigators who scoured the premises where the killing supposedly took place could find no forensic evidence of any kind.

> "That," said Dr. Norton, "is because Lacresha did not kill Jayla."

Jayla was a chronically abused and malnourished child who was dropped off at Lacresha's house by her mother's boyfriend. Dr. Norton believed the child was already severely injured, based on her listless behavior, bruises and other medical evidence. When Jayla was brought to the hospital, doctors tried CPR—about 100 chest compressions per minute for 20 minutes—on the very thin child.

Because Lacresha had carried the little girl to the hospital, she became the suspect. When the tape of her confessions surfaced, it was clear she couldn't even read what she had "confessed." The police had questioned her for hours without her guardians or a lawyer. Finally, they had told her that if she signed the confession, she could go home to her grandma. In an audiotape of the confession, Lacresha reportedly asked "What's that word? 'Home-a-seed'?" No one responded.

As a result, she was sentenced to 25 years, at that point now 12 years old.

In working to publicize the miscarriage of justice in Lacresha's case, McKinney used many of the same tactics as with my daughter's situation: strategizing with her volunteer attorneys, rolling out the media attention aggressively, throwing some smoke and mirrors as to how powerful we could be, embarrassing the state and the prosecutorial offices and generating a coalition of concerned voices. Bob Herbert was critical in bringing Lacresha's plight to light, as he has been in so many other cases of injustice. As a result of Herbert's series, *60 Minutes* gained interest. Ultimately, the pressure forced a reexamination of the case, and Lacresha was released—but not before spending three years in the juvenile-justice system, an experience that robbed her of liberty and possibilities that she can never reclaim.

We always embraced the truism that failure was not an option. The causes were too important for us to fail.

We were determined that Lacresha's story be told—and be told widely and well. It was that same determination that spurred me and Gwen McKinney to start our PR firm. We were ready to compete with the "big boys" in the nation's capital, even though our office was in a church basement in the "'hood" and we had no startup capital. We eventually became a successful firm under the slogan "public relations with a conscience," dedicated to utilizing communications to advance social change.

Whether it was bringing an intransigent Shell Oil Company to the table in a glass-ceiling discrimination case through media coverage, generating attention to former TransAfrica director Randall Robinson's hunger strike to reverse the U.S. policy on Haiti or expressing the human and moral face of President Jean Bertrand Aristide, who had been vilified in the American media, we always embraced the truism that failure was not an option. The causes were too important for us to fail. And so we utilized innovative, creative strategies so our clients' stories could be told in the most effective outlets, from the *New York Times* to *Good Morning America*. We always had to make a way—even if there was no way.

Today, Gwen has continued that tradition building McKinney & Associates perhaps the nation's only African American female-owned firm dedicated to social change. She has remained true to her ethics, never betraying her core principles—the same principles we began with in that church basement. She has soared over the challenges of sexism and racism that still plague us. I cannot count the times we would go to a prospective progressive client and be passed over for far less qualified white-owned firms or be told that yes, we could do the "Black media." In the prospective client's mind, despite our stellar track record of excellent media coverage from the most sought-after press, they considered our most worthy claim to fame would be to secure placement in the "Black press." For a story in the *Washington Post* or a comprehensive media strategy, they presumed they needed a white firm. This is not to say that the Black press, with its noble tradition, is not a most worthy vehicle. However, our skills and savvy should not have confined us to an either-or proposition.

Throughout all the challenges, Gwen has never missed a beat. She has mentored numerous young PR professionals of color. She has courageously continued to build a firm that is often the only powerful voice for the voiceless, a firm that brings justice to the victims of injustice and a firm that uses its exceptional expertise to create a better world.

Busboys & Poets: Roots in the Past and a Vital Role Today

ANDY SHALLAL

Andy Shallal, artist/businessman/bibliophile, has caught lightning in a jar. The founder of the popular gathering place Busboys & Poets started with a vision of bringing vibrant cultural and political voices together on a site rich in African American history. He now runs five restaurants throughout the DC Metropolitan Area, honoring the legacy of great Black authors. They are thriving safe houses for progressive thought, good eating and social change. He talked with Gwen McKinney about his inspiration for Busboys & Poets, the real roots of the Harlem Renaissance and his work with McKinney to stop the corporatization of Washington's neighborhoods.

GM: Busboys & Poets -- an amazing concept. You can come into any of your places on any given evening and find a multicultural stew, a delicious stew, of people and experiences. Your diners, your speakers, your book buyers cross class lines, generations, cultures, races and ethnicities. You got it! How did you do that?

AS: It's got to be intentional. It doesn't just happen. You can't just open a place and have good coffee and good food and expect people of *all* types to come to it. People tend to self-segregate. In order for our place not to be segregated, we had to reach out further, deeper; we had to create programming and events that would bring different kinds of people together and make them all feel at home.

Believe it or not, it starts with the menu. You have to have a menu that is friendly to everyone; that honors traditions. If you're going to have Black patrons coming, for instance, you have to have catfish on that menu. That's a starter. Not every Black person likes catfish, clearly, but seeing it on our menu provides a sense of welcome. It says, "I acknowledge you, I acknowledge your culture." To me, that's basic. Some might shy away from such dishes because they think "Oh, I'm stereotyping, I'm going in an area where I'm not comfortable ..." Since I'm very comfortable talking about race, it is not a problem for me. I also feel comfortable with incorporating non-verbal cues like our menu choices -- intentionally and purposefully into the big picture.

The other key component is the programming. I did my research very carefully. When I was looking for a place to open in this neighborhood, in the U Street corridor, I drove up and down the streets, observing the changes that were underway.

This area used to be called "Black Broadway." It was the epicenter of the Civil Rights Movement. This is literally where the movement sprung up. Across the street from here was the SNCC (Student Nonviolent Coordinating Committee) office. Right around the corner, when Martin Luther King, Jr. was assassinated in 1968, the streets were on fire. There was a People's drug store there where a brick went through a window and suddenly there was turmoil: people running up and down the streets, looting and rioting. All kinds of things took place here during that time. I was a young boy watching this. I saw buildings burning all around DC.

Between then and now it was abandoned for a long time. During the '70s and '80s this area was not a very good neighborhood, there was a lot of drug dealing on the corners.

GM: The powers that be let everything decline to nothing.

AS: Exactly. But then it started coming back after the blight. Finally, when the Metro opened here in 1991, things started changing. And some of those changes were good: the streets were getting cleaned up; people were moving back into this neighborhood. Buildings started going up in the Black Broadway area – the Ellington, the Langston.

One day I was driving and saw that the basement of the Ellington had been occupied by a tanning salon. The building is named after Duke Ellington, one of the greatest Black composers and musicians of all time. For someone to put a tanning salon in this building was not the way to honor the past or the values of this community.

> *I wanted this to be a marker; we were going to continue the grand legacy of this neighborhood.*

So I went looking for that ideal space. When I saw a building going up called "Langston Lofts," I knew that Langston Hughes had to be somewhere in there. I talked with the landlord and tried to figure out how I could lease a space in that apartment building. After much back and forth and lots of turmoil, the landlord and I could not reach an agreement. In the end, I had to buy the whole building from him and do it my way.

I opened a combination restaurant, bookstore and meeting place. I called it Busboys & Poets after the great poet, Langston Hughes, who lived in this city in the 1920s, working as a busboy at the Wardman Park Hotel. I wanted this to be a marker; we were going to continue the grand legacy of this neighborhood.

11

When I dug a little deeper into the neighborhood history, I found out that at this very corner where we're sitting right now, there was an African American community center. On the second floor they used to have open mics on Tuesdays. People would come and read poetry and tell stories. I wanted to make sure that that was brought back. So now we have Tuesday "Open Mic" nights – and it is extremely successful. People are delighted to come here and have their voices heard, in a community that's nurturing and friendly. That's really what this neighborhood is all about. That's what I wanted to create. We renamed the street "Langston Hughes Way" because I wanted to make sure that any tourist driving around would know this is where Langston Hughes walked. This is his way.

There is so much rich history here and the area is still not being honored at the level that it should be. This was the birthplace of the Harlem Renaissance. Howard University is just a few blocks away. W.E.B. DuBois worked here. This is the place where Langston Hughes walked the streets, where Zora Neale Hurston walked [Shallal also opened a restaurant across the street from the first Busboys called Eatonville in 2009, named after Hurston's hometown and the first post-Civil War African-American incorporated town], where Countee Cullen walked, where Duke Ellington walked, where Ella Fitzgerald walked … this is the place, this is it! But over the years, those memories started getting erased, over and over and over again, covered up with a veneer. I really wanted to pull this great legacy out of the earth, from underneath the ground, and bring it back up to the surface. This is what makes the neighborhood vibrant and exciting.

Although many people may be unfamiliar with the Howard Theatre, it was opened right here in 1905, 10 years before the Apollo in Harlem. People don't know the Howard that well, but now it's starting to get renovated. Hopefully its legacy will come back, because for the longest time, people had no idea that *this* was actually the birthplace of the Harlem Renaissance.

GM: You have a fascinating mix of experiences and aspirations. You are Iraqi-American, you studied medicine at Howard University, decided to take off for California to find yourself, and eventually returned to D.C. What about all of this led you to where you are sitting today?

AS: Life is a series of experiences, and I believe that those people who find their stride have gleaned bits and pieces from every experience they've gone through. I had to define me. I had to figure out who I am, and I have been through some key defining moments. I came to the United States at the age of 10. As a young boy, I had to deal with race and its implications in this country. Because I had darker skin than a white person, I was put in a "Black" category. I didn't even know what that meant. I didn't know what "White" meant. I was just me. And here I was in this space where you had to define yourself. The Black girls would look at me and say "what are you?" The White girls would look at me and say "we want nothing to do with you."

So, there I was in a limbo state – not knowing where or how to fit in. But I quickly realized that race is huge in this country: Race determines who gets locked-up, where you get a job, who you end up living with, what neighborhood you live in…amazing! What a concept: the pigment of your skin determines almost everything about you in this country. That was an eye-opening experience for a young immigrant boy.

True, racism is prevalent all over the world. But in this country, there's a special layer because of the legacy of slavery that has not been dealt with, that has not been talked about, that has not been brought to the surface. This continues to dog us. For example, just a couple of years ago we had a mayoral election in this city: two Black men vying with each other for the same office. Yet it was still all about race. One candidate was perceived as the "White" mayor, even though he was Black. The other was perceived as the "Black" mayor, primarily because of his base of support. What is that all about? We have to get beyond this idea, this construct that has been created, that is tied more to power than pigmentation. We have to get beyond that construct and be able to look at each other, not just by the color of our skin, but really by the depth of our character.

Even today the city is so segregated, though, of course, legally it's not supposed to be. Let's take my vantage point from the res-taurant business. It's clear that some restaurants are considered "White" restaurants and then there are the "other" restaurants. Why are most restaurants in the city segregated? This has al-ways baffled me -- the idea that you cannot have Black people and White people eating together at the same table. That is still an unusual sight today, even in 2011.

I felt it was vital to create a space that could break those bar-riers, that could bring people together culturally, aesthetically -- over food. I know how to do food. That's my competency. So I bring people together in this kind of environment, lay it out on the table, literally, and then have people come and figure it out for themselves. Because I do believe that if you create the environment to mix people in a safe, comfortable space, people will be able to move forward and trust one another to develop relationships. Then, maybe someday we may be able to see a whole different world.

GM: McKinney & Associates worked with you during our campaign against Wal-Mart that was dubbed Respect DC. As part of our communications effort, we had to enlist strong voices to speak out about why Wal-Mart should not come to town with its proposed four-store infiltration. You stepped right up, and the passion and authenticity of your voice advanced the overall messaging. You have a successful chain of restaurants stamped with an enviable brand, and you didn't have to get involved in this controversy. Why did you so readily join us?

AS: As someone who has lived in DC for a long time, I've seen a lot of changes take place here. Some of the changes are genuinely good; they respect the traditions of the city. This is important for community involvement. It means that we can have neigh-borhoods that become vibrant, that spring back even after being blighted for so many years. This is our moment for DC to define itself. Things are changing, mostly for the better.

Like you, and others who love this city, I did not want to see something like a Wal-Mart – so generic, gigantic, and non-descript – putting such a huge footprint on the city and altering the landscape of where we live.

Retail plays a vital role in the real identity of a city. Your street-scape, the kind of stores you go to, the places you frequent -- coffee shops, clothing stores, shoe stores -- all of these things shape a neighborhood's look and feel.

This city has gone through moments that were very difficult. We're starting to see the Mom & Pop stores slowly rise above water. In the next couple years, we'll see a flourishing of these types of businesses and BOOM! In comes Wal-Mart and wipes all this effort out. As in so many other communities, they will end up putting it in a worse condition than it was before they laid down their marker. It's been shown over and over again, that's what happens. I didn't want to see that happen to this city.

GM: So, was it a quixotic effort?

AS: Well, you know, it's an effort that's still ongoing. I think the battle's not over. We're still working to see if Wal-Mart, in fact, does come to DC, what we can do to limit its detrimental impact on so many small businesses. And there is still some hope that we can keep Wal-Mart out of the city. The people have to speak up. This should not be seen as poor people against people with means; this is a concern that should embrace every part of the city.

Through the broad-based communications effort, the idea of respecting DC came through loud and clear, I think. A big corporation like Wal-Mart is not coming here because they love DC. They want to suck the blood out of DC. And that's the part that really should concern everyone, no matter what his or her economic status.

GM: We have something else in common, besides our collaboration in the Respect DC campaign. Some 20 years ago, in 1990, in the basement of the Saint Augustine Ecumenical Center at 1419 V Street, just up the street from this Busboys & Poets, our little firm began to ply its trade and dared to start public relations with a conscience.

AS: Wow! Amazing connections!

GM: So from 1419 V Street to 1612 K Street...

AS: Cool, very cool

GM: As you share the rich legacy of this neighborhood and all you have done to preserve it, I feel like I'm part of that history. I was getting chills because it just shows the continuum of time and struggle. I'm not Langston Hughes or Zora Neale Hurston, but this neighborhood is part of my legacy too – my partner Leila McDowell and I walked these streets as we dared to create a different kind of public relations agency, with few resources and a powerful passion for social justice.

So your storytelling gives context to an invaluable part of our anthology of public relations with a conscience. I am very proud about that.

AS: I want to make sure that history is not just covered over, but pulled from underneath the earth. There are spirits underneath us right now that I feel need to be brought out, lifted up. And in order for any kind of an enterprise to be successful, you have to speak to those spirits; you can't ignore them and cover them up. Otherwise, they're going to come back to haunt you! For me, it's an important, sacred thing that we do when we develop any kind of a business with a conscience, any kind of an institution that's going to have long-lasting impact. It has to have a connection, a root into the history of the community that it's coming into and coming from.

Sanctioned Injustice: Fighting Back Against Capital Punishment

DIANN RUST-TIERNEY

I remember working with McKinney & Associates on the case of Gary Graham when I served as the director of the Capital Punishment Project for the American Civil Liberties Union. Graham, who later changed his name to Shaka Sankofa, had been convicted and sentenced to death in 1981 for the murder of Bobby Grant Lambert in a Safeway parking lot in Houston, Texas. After spending almost two decades on death row, his execution was scheduled for June 22, 2000.

On its face, Graham's case might not have been expected to garner the national concern and attention it would later command. Nor might it seem a likely choice to shed light on the complex considerations surrounding the death penalty, one of our country's most vexing legal and moral issues. To many, he might be considered to be exactly the type for which the death penalty was designed. Though he was only a teenager at the time of the Lambert murder, Sankofa had a long and very recent history of serious violent offenses, including a series of armed robberies. It was his arrest for the abduction and rape of a Houston cab driver that prompted police to include Sankofa's arrest photo among the mug shots reviewed by witnesses to Bobby Lambert's murder.

But Shaka Sankofa claimed he was innocent of the crime for which he would be sentenced to death. And there were disturbing questions about the reliability of Sankofa's conviction and death sentence, precisely because he *was* well-known to police and therefore less likely to have his claim of innocence believed.

Sankofa's court-appointed lawyer, Ron Mock, failed to investigate, interview or call alibi witnesses during the trial; he also failed to explore discrepancies among eyewitness testimony in the case. Though not everyone on death row's case is scrutinized, these grave errors by the defense drew the attention of national civil- and human-rights groups.

The ACLU had been asked to support the efforts of the NAACP Legal Defense Fund, Amnesty International USA and the National Coalition to Abolish the Death Penalty because of their grave concerns that race, class and a terribly broken system of justice had conspired to sentence an innocent man to death.

We had our work cut out for us. Executions in Texas at that time were—and even are *now*—a recurring and unsettlingly all-too-frequent event. We needed to garner public attention in order to gain the appropriate oversight of the case. It was not going to be easy. The first meeting of civil-rights, civil-liberties, human-rights and religious organizations focused on the case was a real crossroads. This was when I first realized what an asset Gwen McKinney was going to be to this challenging effort. In a time of great turmoil and heightened emotions, she had a confident and determined demeanor. She listened carefully and skillfully translated the facts and the legal procedures in the case. She instinctively identified the themes and messages that would resonate in the public forum and could best be used to mobilize popular concern and opposition to Shaka Sankofa's execution.

The Sankofa case typified the many flaws inherent in the administration of capital punishment: the influence that race plays in the likelihood of a death sentence and execution, particularly when—as was the case here—the defendant is black and the victim is white; the quality of legal representation and the weight that has on whether a defendant receives a death sentence; and the risk of wrongful executions, particularly when race is a factor.

The other key question raised by this case was whether Shaka Sankofa, who was 17 years old at the time of his arrest, should even have been *eligible* for the death penalty. Indeed, the Supreme Court decided, just five years after his execution, that to subject juvenile offenders like Sankofa to the death penalty was a violation of the Constitution's protection against "cruel and unusual punishment."

I watched Gwen and her team—with the same cool determination as in that first meeting—deftly pull together the structure of a coordinated campaign to publicize the injustice that we firmly believed was about to occur in Texas. As an added boost to our efforts, Gwen's long history of work and connections to high-level civil-rights and political leadership allowed us to put Sankofa's plight before these leaders quickly and garner their support and the assistance of their networks.

Even in Texas, the pace of death sentencing and executions has slowed significantly.

With Gwen's help, the growing coalition of organizations working to save Shaka Sankofa from execution took advantage of newly discovered evidence to highlight the case in the media and bring more people into the effort to save his life. Two witnesses who said that Shaka Sankofa was not the person they saw kill Bobby Lambert had been discouraged from testifying. We were able to widely publicize this new evidence. We took every avenue available to us. Newspaper ads, press conferences, rallies, church meetings and media appearances were our currency. We enlisted the reverends Jesse Jackson and Al Sharpton, Bianca Jagger, Danny Glover, Ramsey Clark and Rubin Hurricane Carter. They were among the many influential and everyday citizens who lent their names and invested considerable time to the effort. Thousands of people sent letters and called the governor and the Board of Pardons and Parole.

In the end, we failed to save Shaka Sankofa. He was executed by the state of Texas on June 22, 2000. But our effort to save his life brought some victories as well. We were able to drive home how deeply flawed the system was in Texas—and, indeed, in *every* state that continues to cling to capital punishment. We planted the seeds for long-lasting coalition efforts. And we identified and illuminated a shared sense of how the system of justice has failed not only criminal defendants but witnesses, jurors and victims.

Today we are beginning to see the long-term effects of our work to abolish capital punishment. Illinois is the most recent state to repeal its death-penalty statute—because of the very concerns raised in Shaka Sankofa's case. Even in Texas, the pace of death sentencing and executions has slowed significantly. Elsewhere, the death penalty is clearly waning, with at least a half-dozen states within reach of ending the practice. I have no doubt that the early, determined effort, buoyed by the talent and commitment of Gwen McKinney and her team, had an even greater impact than we could have imagined at the time.

A New Way of Life: From Prison to Advocacy

SUSAN BURTON (AS TOLD TO MONIQUE BRACKETT)

It was Thanksgiving weekend, 2009. I was in bed with the flu, half-asleep, when the phone rang. It was my good friend Saúl Sarabia, a law professor at the University of California, Los Angeles (UCLA).

"I'm watching this *CNN Heroes* show, and I'm so inspired," he said. "I think you're a hero, and I'm going to nominate you. So don't be surprised when CNN calls for an interview."

He then asked a series of questions in rapid succession: When was my child killed? When did I open the houses? Which one first? And how many women had been through them since the beginning? I gave him fuzzy, fevered answers, rolled over and went back to sleep. When I got a call a few days later from a CNN producer, you could have knocked me over with a feather.

But let me backtrack a little.

I was born in Los Angeles, in the Aliso Village housing project. Life wasn't easy. As a child, I was sexually and physically abused. I dropped out of high school and had a baby. The death of my son was my final breaking point; I went on a downward spiral of drugs and imprisonment. After being caught in the criminal-justice system for almost two decades, I broke free and founded A New Way of Life Reentry Project to help other women like me. Since 1998, I have helped more than 600 women returning home from prison. I offer them shelter, safety, inspiration and support as they seek to rebuild their lives.

A New Way of Life has given me a sense of purpose to make a mark in the world. It demonstrates that if we provide services to people coming home from prisons and jails, they can break free from cycling in and out of the system. Countless times, I have witnessed the joy of a mother and her child reunited. It fills my heart to see them bond in a safe and supportive environment where they can thrive as a family and live happy and productive lives. These moments give me strength when times get hard.

When I first opened my home to women returning from prison, I knew I was helping to give them a head start, but I truly didn't expect to receive so much from them. Belief, faith, hope—that's what our house gave birth to more than anything.

And times *do* get hard. Doubts creep in. Once, I was trying to get some sleep in a little corner of my house and thinking that the circumstances we *all* faced were so overwhelming that it just might be too much to bear. I think every formerly incarcerated person goes through this because of a combination of things: the blatant discrimination we face on a daily basis; the never knowing what's going to happen next week, next month or next year; the understanding that what we have is actually not enough to even survive and the battling of an old way of being that might cause harm or break a law. The struggles of reentry are more than people should have to endure. They're unfair and continued punishments.

The reality of our daily lives can be daunting, but the community, camaraderie and family—building blocks for A New Way of Life—kept me going through all the doubt, fear and uncertainty. When I first opened my home to women returning from prison, I knew I was helping to give them a head start, but I truly didn't expect to receive so much from them: belief, faith and hope; that's what our house gave birth to more than anything.

When A New Way of Life opened in 1998, my friend Saúl was among the first to embrace the fact that I was inviting women from prison to stay in my home. He got it; he actually got it more than I got it, and with that, he taught me. He was working for the Community Coalition of South Los Angeles and invited me to a meeting there. Later, after visiting the women, he was sold on my vision. He encouraged me to hang in there, because he knew it was tough. And it was very tough. He motivated me, connected me with resources and was a source of sheer inspiration.

Now, back to that phone call from the CNN producer. She said that I had been nominated as a "CNN Hero" and proceeded with a few questions. My initial thought was Wow! Just to get the call was huge. But it didn't take long for the never-ending concerns of A New Way of Life—dealing with new arrivals, raising funds, making sure the children had enough clothes and campaigning for former prisoners to register to vote—to quickly push daydreams to the back of my consciousness. I had almost forgotten about that call when, months later, CNN returned. This time, they dropped the bomb that I had been selected as one of their 2010 Top 10 Heroes. This was so far beyond my wildest dreams. I had been selected from nominees from all over the world, and I had a chance at becoming the CNN Top Hero, an honor bestowed to the winner of the most online votes. What it said to me was that the broad public—even a mainstream news outlet—supports reentry work in a real way. And it put me into another category: while I accept who I am and what I do, it said that the world accepts it, too.

I was still trying to take everything in. A whirlwind of events swirled around me as the excitement of soliciting votes to be the Top Hero became my mission. I hosted "vote parties," for hours at a time, where supporters came into one of my homes, got on their laptops and voted. My friends created e-mail blasts that went all around the world. We sought support from universities, churches and social-justice organizations. I went and spoke to whoever would listen. We distributed thousands of postcards. I even used my birthday to rally votes and asked everyone to vote 59 times on that day because I was turning 59. On top of my own outreach, I began to receive speaking invitations and awards from across the country, including an invitation from the NAACP and Harvard University's Gleitsman Citizen Activist Award. These tactics all spotlighted the CNN nomination and the need for people to vote. My life had been forever changed.

Prodded by Saúl, UCLA students also got onboard to promote the nomination. Students held a campus-wide voting campaign and allowed me to come speak. One UCLA student developed a method to cast the maximum number of votes in one minute, which was demonstrated and broadcast to other students. "Vote for Susan Burton as CNN's Top Hero of 2010" was plastered across the campus, and students pledged to secure one million votes in the last 24 hours of voting.

But the most fabulous support came from McKinney & Associates. I felt so lucky to be connected, because Gwen McKinney really understood the importance of A New Way of Life and how the CNN spotlight could help us expand our work and help more women. McKinney helped me to get into places that I could never have approached, like National Public Radio. They arranged television interviews and placements in leading newspapers like the *Los Angeles Times*. I can't even remember it all because the media outreach coordinated through McKinney was so extensive. They created a vibrant Facebook fan page for me and constant Twitter feeds. Their e-campaign was so incredible that CNN called to ask me who they were, because the social-marketing campaign was so widespread; McKinney had totally impressed CNN with the online presence they had created for me.

My experience with the media was positive because I was prepared. From working with McKinney, I was clear on how to deliver my message, give my pitch and stay focused during interviews. McKinney also helped me to distinguish which media were really interested in my work and which just wanted to pick a fight. I learned not to get engaged by the ones who were looking for a sore spot or a wound. For example, a few interviewers wanted to get into specifics of the crimes that had been committed by the women in the house. But *this* story was not about the crimes—it was about redemption. I actually sat down with women in my homes to give them media talking points and an understanding on how to answer questions and where not to go. It was a little puzzling to them, as it was to me in the beginning, but with McKinney's guidance, we worked through it.

Most importantly, Gwen McKinney took the time to help me reflect on the depth of my experiences and bring to the surface that miraculous ability that enabled me to recover and overcome my past. Gwen gave me the image of bridges: the bridges that I have helped create, so many different bridges leading out to so many different areas to be traveled by so many women. I use that analogy a lot when I talk about what A New Way of Life means to me and to the women who come into my home. My own personal bridge led me to the 2010 *CNN Heroes* taping as an honoree. And although I didn't receive the top hero award, the experience helped me understand that I was already a winner.

After being thrust into the international spotlight, A New Way of Life has received a staggering amount of attention and support from local and national government, individuals and foundations. This outpouring validates all of our struggles, hard times and challenges. I hope that the recognition made possible by the *CNN Heroes* campaign will give others like me the hope that they can make their own mark and the confidence that they won't be shunned because of their backgrounds.

Months after the awards ceremony, I am still trying to manage the influx of emails, phone calls, requests and inquiries; I still haven't gotten through them all. I have heard from people all over the nation who want to start reentry projects. I actually learned from the media campaign that people have started reentry projects out of their homes and apartments. One female minister in Colorado started a home in a gated community after hearing about my work. I never thought my story would inspire so many.

Before I met Gwen, my definition of public relations was much shallower. But I learned a lot about the media from Gwen, who has a broad and deep understanding of the best way to get a message across—she thinks huge! So I've learned quite a bit during the process of working with her and seeing the results. And I'm sure there's a whole lot more to learn. I feel really, really lucky to have met her, and now I consider her a friend. I also learned a lot from the way she viewed my work: she looked at our effort and saw such deep value in it. And I appreciate that; I really do.

We all have dreams. And when you believe strongly in one, don't be afraid to seek help in actually birthing and realizing the full potential of that dream. McKinney was perfect in helping me to fully realize my dream in the most fruitful way.

I wouldn't change one thing about the experience that started with a phone call from my friend Saúl on Thanksgiving 2009. Well, maybe *one* thing: if I could do it all over, when speaking at the CNN awards taping, I would have sent a message to President Obama to create more resources and programs for reentry.

Cruel and Unequal

MICHELLE ALEXANDER

Michelle Alexander's groundbreaking book, "The New Jim Crow: Mass Incarceration in the Age of Colorblindness," also took the civil rights world by storm. Speaking around the country—from university classrooms to national television broadcasts to community meetings of formerly incarcerated people—she has inspired a new public dialogue on today's hidden racial reality and spurred a growing movement against a criminal justice system designed to disempower communities of color.

McKinney & Associates is honored to partner with Alexander to amplify her call to arms via mass media and social marketing. We are one in the conviction that confronting the cages and castes of this century is the ultimate civil-rights struggle.

Following is a taste of her innovative thinking, from an article originally published in "Sojourners" magazine.

Blacks and whites use drugs at about the same rate, yet African Americans are 10 times as likely to be imprisoned for drug offenses. The unbalanced effects of the "war on drugs."

So much about our racial reality today is little more than a mirage. The promised land of racial equality quivers just out of our reach in the barren desert of our new, "colorblind" political landscape. It looks so good from a distance: Barack Obama, our nation's first black president, standing behind a podium in the Rose Garden looking handsome, dignified, and in charge. Flip the channel, and there's the whole Obama family exiting Air Force One, waving to the crowd—a gorgeous black family living in the White House, cheered by the world.

The members of the undercaste are largely invisible to those of us who have jobs, live in decent neighborhoods and zoom around on freeways, passing by the virtual and literal prisons in which they live.

Drive a few blocks from the White House and you find the other America. You find you're still in the desert, dying of thirst, wondering what wrong turn was made and how you managed to miss the promised land, though you reached for it with all your might.

A vast new racial undercaste now exists in America, though [its] plight is rarely mentioned. Obama won't mention it; the Tea Party won't mention it; media pundits would rather talk about anything else. The members of the undercaste are largely invisible to those of us who have jobs, live in decent neighborhoods, and zoom around on freeways, passing by the virtual and literal prisons in which they live.

But here are the facts: There are more African American adults under correctional control today—in prison or jail, on probation or parole—than were enslaved in 1850, a decade before the Civil War began. In major urban areas such as Chicago, Obama's hometown, the *majority* of working-age African American men have criminal records and are thus subject to legalized discrimination for the rest of their lives. Millions of people in the United States, primarily poor people of color, are denied the very rights supposedly won in the civil-rights movement: the right to vote, to serve on juries and to be free from discrimination in employment, housing, access to education and public benefits. Branded "criminals" and "felons," such people now find themselves relegated to a permanent second-class status. They live in a parallel social universe: the other America, where they will stay for the rest of their lives.

We, as a nation, are in deep denial about how this came to pass. On the rare occasions when the existence of "them"—the others, the ghetto dwellers, those locked up and locked out—is publicly acknowledged, standard excuses are trotted out. We're told black culture, bad schools, poverty and broken homes are to blame. Almost no one admits: we declared war. We declared a war on the most vulnerable people in our society and then blamed them for the wreckage.

And yet that is precisely what we did. The so-called War on Drugs has driven the quintupling of our prison population in a few short decades. The vast majority of the startling increase in incarceration in America is traceable to the arrest and imprisonment of poor people of color for nonviolent, drug-related offenses. Families have been torn apart, and young lives shattered, as parents grieve the loss of loved ones to the system, often hiding their grief under a cloak of shame.

Politicians claim that the enemy in this war is a thing—drugs—not a group of people. The facts prove otherwise.

Studies consistently show that people of all colors *use and sell* drugs at remarkably similar rates, yet in some states African American men have been admitted to prison on drug charges at a rate up to 57 times higher than white men. In some states, 80 to 90 percent of all drug offenders sent to prison have been African Americans. The rate of Latino imprisonment has been staggering, as well. Although the majority of illegal drug users and dealers are white, three-fourths of all people imprisoned for drug offenses have been black and Latino.

This war has been waged almost exclusively in poor, ghetto communities. For those who are tempted to imagine that the goal of the war has been to root out violent offenders or drug kingpins, think again. Federal funding flows to those state and local law enforcement agencies that dramatically boost the sheer volume of drug arrests; it's a numbers game. Agencies don't get rewarded for bringing down drug bosses or arresting violent offenders. They're rewarded in cash for arresting people en masse. Ghetto communities are swept for the low-hanging fruit—which generally means young people hanging out the street corner, walking to school or the subway, or driving around with friends. They're stopped and searched for any reason or no reason at all. In 2005, for example, four out of five drug arrests were for possession; only one of five was for sales. And in the 1990s—the period of the most drastic expansion of the drug war—nearly 80 percent of the increase in drug arrests were for possession of marijuana, a drug less harmful than alcohol and tobacco and at least as prevalent in middle-class white communities and college campuses as it is in poor communities of color.

But it is in the poverty-stricken, racially segregated ghettos, where the War on Poverty has been abandoned and factory jobs have disappeared, that the drug war has been waged with ferocity. SWAT teams are deployed here; buy-bust operations are concentrated here; drug raids of schools and housing projects occur here; stop-and-frisk operations are conducted on these streets. If such tactics were employed in middle-class white neighborhoods or on college campuses, there would be public outrage; the war would end overnight. But here in the ghetto, the stops, searches, sweeps and mass arrests are treated as an accepted fact of life, like the separate water fountains of an earlier era.

By the millions, people are arrested and marched into courtrooms in shackles. When released, they're stripped of their right to vote and their right to serve on juries. Discrimination against them is officially legal. Barred from public housing and denied even food stamps, millions find they are deemed unworthy of the nation's care or concern. Jobless, hungry, without shelter and riddled with shame, they're trapped in the desert wasteland. The majority of those released from prison return within months of their release, unable to make it on the outside.

It is impossible to imagine anything like this happening if the enemy in the drug war were white, as economist Glenn Loury observes in his book *The Anatomy of Racial Inequality*. Can we envision a system that would enforce drug laws almost exclusively against young white men and largely ignore drug crime among young black men? Can we imagine large majorities of young white men being rounded up for minor drug offenses, placed under the control of the criminal justice system, labeled felons and subjected to a lifetime of discrimination, scorn and exclusion? No, we cannot. If such a thing occurred, as Loury says, it would make us wonder "what had gone wrong, not with them, but us"—all of us. The large-scale criminalization of white men would "disturb us at our core. So the question becomes What disturbs us?" What upsets us? Or, more to the point: Whom do we care about?

An answer to the last question may be found by considering the drastically different manner that we, as a nation, responded to drunk driving in the mid-1980s, as compared to crack cocaine. The drug war was initiated by political elites; only much later did ordinary people identify drug crime as an issue of extraordinary concern. In contrast, the movement to crack down on drunk drivers was a broad-based, bottom-up movement, led most notably by mothers whose families were shattered by deaths caused by drunk driving. Throughout the 1980s, drunk driving was a regular topic in the media, and the term "designated driver" became part of the American lexicon.

At the close of the decade, drunk drivers were responsible for approximately 22,000 deaths annually, and overall alcohol-related deaths were close to 100,000 a year. By contrast, during the same time period, there were no prevalence statistics at all on crack, much less crack-related deaths. In fact, the number of deaths related to all illegal drugs combined was tiny compared to the number of deaths caused by drunk drivers. The total of all drug-related deaths, whether from AIDS, drug overdose, or the violence associated with the illegal drug trade, was estimated at 21,000 annually—less than the number of deaths directly caused by drunk drivers, and a small fraction of the number of alcohol-related deaths that occur every year.

In response to growing concern—fueled by advocacy groups such as MADD and by the media coverage of drunk-driving fatalities—most states adopted tougher laws to punish drunk driving. Numerous states now have some type of mandatory sentencing for this offense—typically two days in jail for a first offense and two to 10 days for a second offense.

New laws governing crack cocaine were passed at the same time legislatures were "getting tough" on drunk drivers. But notice the contrast: while drunk driving results in a few days in prison, possession of a tiny amount of crack carries a mandatory minimum sentence of five years in federal prison. In fact, some people are serving *life sentences* for minor drug offenses. In *Harmelin v. Michigan*, the U.S. Supreme Court upheld a sentence of life imprisonment for a defendant with no prior convictions who tried to sell 23 ounces of crack cocaine. The court concluded that life imprisonment was not "cruel and unusual punishment" in violation of the Eighth Amendment, despite the fact that no other developed country in the world imposes life imprisonment for a first-time drug offense.

The vastly different sentences afforded drunk drivers and drug offenders speaks volumes regarding who is viewed as disposable—someone to be purged from the body politic—and who is not. Drunk drivers are predominately white and male. White men comprised 78 percent of the arrests for drunk driving when the new mandatory minimums for the offense were being adopted. They are generally charged with misdemeanors and typically receive sentences involving fines, license suspension and community service.

Although drunk driving carries a far greater risk of violent death than the use or sale of illegal drugs, the societal response to drunk drivers has generally emphasized keeping the person functional and in society while attempting to respond to the dangerous behavior through treatment and counseling. People charged with drug offenses, though, are disproportionately poor people of color. They are typically charged with felonies and sentenced to prison. If and when they're released, they become members of the undercaste, no longer locked up, but locked out—for the rest of their lives.

This is not a problem begging merely for policy reform. Much more is required of us. If we fail, as a nation, to awaken to the basic humanity of all those cycling in and out of prison today, and if we fail to commit ourselves to ending mass incarceration, future generations will judge us harshly. A human-rights nightmare is occurring on our watch.

We must do more than bring water to those stranded in the desert. We must act with courage and tell the truth about what is happening in the other America. In the words of Cornel West, "justice is what love looks like in public." If we aim to show love, we must be willing to work for justice.

Cruel and Unequal. By Michelle Alexander. *Sojourners*, February 2011 (Vol. 40, No. 2, pp. 16). Cover.

(Source:http://www.sojo.net/index.cfm?action=magazine.article&issue=soj11 02&article=cruel-and-unequal)

Asian American Advocacy:
A Place at the Table

A VOICE IN THE DEBATE

Karen Narasaki

In the world of McKinney & Associates, once a client, always a client. While the firm has not had Karen Narasaki and the Asian American Justice Center (AAJC) on its roster in recent years, McKinney will continue to share the legacy of AAJC and forever claim association with the organization's unique and important voice. AAJC now enjoys a stellar 20-year history. For most of that time — 17 years — Narasaki has been at the helm. She has personified the organization's achievements, woven from a rich canvass institutionally and personally. This conversation with Karen Narasaki and Gwen McKinney provides a capsule.

GM: The Asian American Justice Center (AAJC) has witnessed many milestones, but not alone. McKinney & Associates was actually there even before this organization had its current title. We helped transition the brand from the National Asian Pacific American Legal Consortium to the Asian American Justice Center. McKinney is proudly a shareholder in AAJC's success.

We invested in defining moments. For instance, in the release of the Annual Asian American Anti-Violence Audits, McKinney helped to catalogue a grave human rights travesty and secure public attention that the issue deserved over five successive years. We delivered media training at the inaugural conference of your Community Partners Network, which would expand to become a formation of grassroots advocates from coast to coast. We contributed to the sustained push for visibility and against stereotypes of Asian Americans and other people of color in mass media. McKinney crafted and helped AAJC release its first media score card on fair reflections of Asian Americans in media, especially on television and in popular culture. And we were there to advance the campaign with AAJC and a coalition of civil rights leaders who won reauthorization of the Voting Rights Act, expanded the debate around affirmative action, took on national immigration policies and amplified the importance of an accurate and inclusive Census count.

This is the table-setting for our conversation, Karen. With so many achievements, some not even mentioned here, if you could cite just one issue that stands out — victory or challenge — what would that be?

KN: First, I thank you, Gwen, for actually helping us to achieve the most fundamental part of our goal, which was to give voice to the Asian American community. When we started 20 years ago, we were invisible as a community. We were not at the table. We were not even thought to have issues. And the goal of the AAJC, from the beginning, was to raise the profile of our community and to try to dispel the myths that surrounded our extremely diverse community.

The most important victory — and there were so many — I believe was the Voting Rights Act extension in 2006. For a long time we felt that there was not an understanding that the Voting Rights Act not only helped African Americans, but also helped Latinos, Native Americans and Asian Americans.

We knew that the reauthorization was not going to be easy. We knew that if we were successful in getting legislation passed to reauthorize, it would be challenged in court.

So how we talked about reauthorizing a law that was over 40 years old, trying to explain to the American public why it was still vitally needed, was going to be a big challenge. On top of that, to bring together these different voices, and make sure that each of our communities understood the issues that each of us was facing, this was going to be critical to winning that battle.

We worked across racial lines and trained everyone together; did media briefings together; did hearings together, rather than as separate communities. I would be talking about how the then recent efforts to suppress the vote of American Indians in South Dakota were similar to the games played in the South against African Americans. The NAACP Legal Defense Fund advocate would be talking about language barriers for Asian Americans. At the end, because we understood each other's issues, we were able to withstand any efforts to play communities against each other and win passage with close to a unanimous vote.

The joint media briefings were your idea, which resulted in stories by African American reporters about voter suppression efforts in Bayou ala Batre against Vietnamese Americans. I loved the cross pollination.

GM: That was significant, the point you make that 30 years ago the Asian American community was not even considered a community. That in itself shows how time and circumstances changed the landscape, placing you in the center of this struggle.

One of the things that you have done, personally and through your institutional mantle, is myth-busting. There is a unique and singular tone in your voice. You worked hard to explode myths and unify struggles. First, staring down the myth of the "model minority" that often characterizes Asian Americans. This was done in two ways: by your example and the work of the organization. Can you speak to that value?

KN: We knew from the very beginning that one of the biggest challenges for the community was to even get people in the progressive movement, much less in the broader public, to understand that we were a community that had struggles. There was this myth that Asians were all doing well in school, that we didn't have poverty, that we really faced no issues of racial discrimination. So we started with doing a report on hate crimes against Asian Americans. We felt that was something that cut across all of our different ethnic groups within the community, but also would resonate with everyone else. How could you dispute the question of whether there was still discrimination in the face of the quite horrible hate crimes that were happening when we started? The AAJC was actually born out of the fact that several Asians had been murdered in hate crimes, and from the lack of official or public response to those hate crimes. So we felt that was really an important beginning for us.

The second goal was to get involved in the affirmative action debate. We were very concerned about the myth that somehow Asians weren't helped by affirmative action, but even more alarmed by the myth that we were *hurt* by affirmative action. We felt that it was very dangerous that other people were speaking on our behalf, who in fact didn't really understand or care about our community and were trying to use us as a wedge against other minority communities.

I benefitted personally from affirmative action. I went to a blue collar high school where the vast majority of kids did not go on to a four year college. My father had high aspirations for me and pushed me to apply to an Ivy League school even though our high school guidance counselors were unable to even tell me what I needed to do. Yale had been co-ed for barely a decade and had very few minorities at the time. Without affirmative action efforts there, I would not have been given serious consideration because of the high school I attended. I think diversity is so important in schools. You can read about discrimination and different cultures but it is different when you know the people who experienced it.

GM: And you did an excellent job of keeping wedge politics out of the equation. Can you speak more about the diversity of the community? What is the multi-tiered, multi-hued face of Asian Americans in this country?

KN: Our community has been very much shaped by waves of immigration and the xenophobic responses to those waves. Asians have actually been in the United States since the 1700s, when Filipinos jumped off Spanish galleys in the South. We were brought into work when slavery ended; first Chinese, then there was a reaction against them; then Japanese were brought in and there was a reaction against them. With each wave, there was a different xenophobic response.

It wasn't until the 1965 Immigration Act that we regard as part of the Civil Rights trilogy of laws — because it ended the racial quotas and said our nation can no longer discriminate based on race as to who gets to come to this country — that the doors opened to Asian immigrants. It's led to over two dozen nationalities, and with each country, within itself there's ethnic diversity. Indians, for example, are Sikh and Hindi and Gujarati, among other identities. Filipinos are made up of many ethnic groups; Chinese as well.

We span many languages, religions and cultures. But what brings us together as a community is the issue of how immigration affects us; discrimination if you're not a Christian; issues of language barriers. We may speak many different languages, but the issue that unites us is the lack of assistance and services to help us learn English; and beyond that, to overcome barriers when we're still in the learning stages. So there are many things that tie us together even though there's a lot of diversity within our communities.

The challenge with immigration is that our country has a love-hate relationship with it. We pride ourselves on being a nation of immigrants, and yet we have this history of waves of xenophobia.

The thing that we had to overcome was home-country politics, because we're coming from a region where there are centuries of conflict, within countries and between Asian countries. So what we've managed to do is leave those issues on the side and work with Asian communities to say, "In the United States, numbers are what matter. After all, when someone is beating an Asian American in a hate crime, it isn't because they actually know what that person's actual ethnicity is. To so many Americans, we are forever foreign. I'm fourth generation Japanese American but people still ask me what country I'm from and compliment me on my English. We have to work together in order to make sure that our communities have the opportunities and overcome the barriers that they confront."

GM: The immigration debate has been a centerpiece of your work, especially over the last decade. You've been intensely involved in the leadership. Where are things now? What would you say, looking at where you were five years ago to where we are today? And I know there's been a lot of ebbs and flows, but how do you assess the struggle?

KN: The challenge with immigration is that our country has a love-hate relationship with it. We pride ourselves on being a nation of immigrants, and yet we have this history of having waves of xenophobia. That's continued even to today — and we're at what I hope is the *height* of a xenophobic reaction — right now with the passage of horrible immigration laws at the state level, like with Alabama, where they are literally trying to keep immigrant kids from attending school.

In the Asian community immigration affects us more than any other community. For example, 60 percent of the Asian community is still foreign born; only 30 percent of the Latino community is foreign born. So anything that has to do with your rights — whether you're a citizen or not — and how immigration laws are applied, who gets to come in, it's going to disproportionately affect our community. What we managed to do over the last 20 years is to make sure that Asians are actually at the table when the debate is happening and when decisions are getting made.

GM: Well that actually brings me to a question you've kind of answered. One of the real challenges and unique charges of AAJC was to create a Pan-Asian front, which is not easy. You addressed this a bit. How were you successful forging Pan-Asian unity? How were you able to do it, especially with the disparate and wide range of people and cultures that you're trying to fuse together?

KN: When I was growing up, people thought of Asians as just the Chinese, Japanese, maybe Filipino. But our community has grown immensely, shaped by refugees who have come from Southeast Asia — from places like Laos and Cambodia and Vietnam — and then in the 80s and 90s we had waves of immigration coming for education and employment opportunities — from Korea, and then from India and Bangladesh and other parts of South Asia.

After 9/11, in fact, I often got asked the question, "Are Indians Asian?" And the answer is "Yes, of course." You can see the breadth of our community in the kinds of issues we face; 9/11 raised a whole different set of issues affecting a significant percentage of Muslim countries. What draws us together is that the U.S. is historically a Judeo-Christian country, you know, open, committed to freedom of religion, but now tested fully on that issue. Sikhs are not Muslim but because their religious practices call for men to wear beards and turbans, they bore a lot of the backlash. In fact, the first hate murder in the backlash after 9/11 was of a Sikh.

Are we really open? Is this really a place where you can have so many diverse religions side by side? It's been one of the ways that Asians have been discriminated against, because many of us are not Christian. At the same time, many of us are. One of the things we learned in bringing the Asian American community together is you really have to start with where people enter. So, they come in with whatever their ethnicity is first, or their religion, and we help them organize first on that level. And then we get them together with other communities and they see that, in fact, they have shared challenges. And they begin to see the power of working together.

The Community Partners Network is one of the things that helped us to do that. We started to identify on the local level where there are emerging leaders and their communities. And then we brought them together at a conference —I believe McKinney & Associates was there helping to do media training as well — and it was so exciting because people were able to see that they had generational issues more than ethnic issues. The younger people from different ethnic backgrounds were saying, "Hey, the older leaders won't let us help lead…" and learned it was not just their immediate community, it was a generational question, and there were people who had tried different things that they could try. We don't need to reinvent the wheel. And so that's been very satisfying work. Once we've put together a more Pan-Asian sense, then we've brought them together with Latinos and African Americans and other communities where they can see the issues they share and the dreams they share, and the goals that every community, every family wants to meet. This helps them to see when they work together, they can become an overwhelming force.

We're a civil rights organization and I feel we have to walk the walk. But also, I really do believe that in diversity there is strength.

GM: That actually brings me to something else. Karen, you have always lived racial justice. That's a remarkable hallmark of your organization, from your executive assistant to the policy analysts, to the designers, to the people who help to shape your public voice and image — you live diversity. You hired an African American and woman-owned firm in the 1990s, at a time that I'm sure, within your community, people were promoting Asian communications professionals, or Whites, or someone other than this small, but bold African American firm. Your staff and partners strike a pose of what diversity is supposed to be. Why has this been so important to you?

KN: We're a civil rights organization and I feel we have to walk the walk. But also, I really do believe that in diversity there is strength. We learn a lot from people who aren't Asian American because they're seeing it from a different perspective. Sometimes it's because, for example, African Americans have seen a lot of the issues we're seeing for the first time and learned lessons along the way and have been very open in saying to us, "Oh, we dealt with that a decade ago; we tried this, don't go there; this is what seems to work..." And so we actually learn from each other. This makes our work stronger, and it makes our impact stronger. Because we're an organization that is trying to speak to the broader public, trying to make sure that other communities understand what we're trying to say about our needs and our aspirations, it's important to have evidence. We can draw from our staff, who tell us, "You know, that's not going to resonate in our community." Or, "This story resonates because this is how it happens in our community."

We hired McKinney & Associates because we saw a lot of mainstream firms just didn't get race. And they weren't willing to take the time to really dig deep and understand a very complicated community that was just starting out, trying to figure out "how do we put a face on a community?" Well, first we need to put a face on the organization and help that be a voice. How do we do that? And we are who we've become in the last 20 years because of all the great advice and support and training that we got from Gwen and her team.

GM: Oh, that's so gratifying to hear.

Karen you have done an exquisite job of answering my questions before I even ask them.

Some closing thoughts. This is your last year in this position. It's bittersweet. Everyone is sad that you're leaving, but happy because we know you will continue to do great things. Through your work and tenure, you have demonstrated that voice matters. Please speak to your voice, to the institutional voice, and to where you want to carry it from here.

KN: My personal mission has been around making sure that people are treated with dignity and justice. Gwen, you know that my family background is that my parents were interned during World War II because they were Japanese American, even though they were born in this country. And that was a very object lesson for our community. The lesson learned was: We have to speak up. We have to be able to tell our own story, and in fact, it's unreasonable to expect that other Americans are going to understand us if we don't stand up and tell our story. And what was important was to get help in trying to figure out how to do that effectively; how to magnify that voice. That's what I've been excited to do with AAJC. It's not been about AAJC being the voice for the Asian American community, but about AAJC being able to empower Asian Americans across the country to be their own voice. That's what I hope is our legacy.

We are launching a legacy fund in my name as I leave AAJC to hopefully expand upon the cross racial work that I began here. In 2000, I said that this century would be about who gets to be treated as fully American. The demographic changes and further globalization of our economy has super-charged ugly debates over immigration and whether we've really overcome the color line. I'm interested in pursuing that question,

The fund will be used by AAJC to support the work that I've been most closely identified with. In addition to the work in pushing for a more fair and sensible immigration system, I've spent the last decade trying to increase and improve the depictions of Asian Americans and other minorities on television and on film. Again, it is about more Americans understanding and sharing our stories. Popular media has such power to either reinforce or break down stereotypes. I want to make sure that AAJC continues to be at the cutting edge of communications in ensuring our stories are seen and heard and that debates over issues like immigration are about facts, not fears.

From Art Files to Zip Files

RICHARD MONTGOMERY

Richard Montgomery has been a recurring feature of McKinney & Associates for almost two decades. An "imagineer" in his own right, he has worked with scores of history makers, welding his background in architecture and his passion for creative design to construct visual imagery that is both engaging and thought provoking.

Looking back over my 20-year career, it is amazing to realize that so little of what we see today is a 100 percent original idea; everything today is an amalgamation of what has preceded it. We are still dealing with the same colors in the natural-light spectrum, the same 26 letters in the alphabet and variations of the same typefaces Johannes Gutenberg used when he created the printing press centuries ago. Today's advances in technology have made it easier to communicate ideas creatively. This technology enables us to do things we never dreamed of before—and to do them better and faster and disseminate them on a vast scale. The main change we as designers now face is how to use these same elements in a way that is effectively portrayed on paper as well as on video screens and other digital devices. The craft, by itself, is not much different from what we learned in school; however, there are many other things that we *don't* learn in school that are important to understand in order to be successful in this field.

Today's advances in technology have made it easier to communicate ideas creatively.

One lesson I had to learn early was that, sometimes—let's say *often*—in this business of influencing social change, you are going to work with a client that lacks the resources necessary to carry the project to fruition. Many times McKinney & Associates found ourselves giving more to a project than we would gain, simply because these projects dealt with values this firm was built on. Even after the client's budget reached its limit, we still provided those services, because we believed our work could make a difference. *That's* what sets us apart from other agencies. And precisely this commitment to "public relations with a conscience" has kept us going for more than 20 years.

I have enjoyed myriad opportunities that stretched my imagination, even on work for an entity as huge and as bureaucratic as the federal government. My first McKinney project was to develop branding for the National Institutes of Health's African American Study on Kidney Disease) campaign—the federal government's first clinical trial probing the links between kidney disease and hypertension in African Americans. It was 1993, and the shadows of the Tuskegee experiments still loomed large (beginning in the 1930s, Black men were human guinea pigs in the study of syphilis over decades); the NIH project leaders knew that understandable barriers to reaching African American participants would impede the project's success. The AASK project required McKinney to employ innovative strategies to encourage the target group to participate in the study. We came up with a wide range of recruitment strategies including celebrity endorsements, promotions at historically Black colleges and universities and engaging brand imagery.

One of the most unusual government projects I worked on was with the Department of Homeland Security shortly after it was created. The DHS was established just a year after the tragic attacks of September 11, 2001, and was the largest reorganization of the federal government since the Cold War—bringing together 200,000 employees from 22 different departments under one roof. This massive reorganization meant that there were a massive number of new protocols and requirements that had to be established and followed—by people who had never worked together before. The information-technology (IT) component was a critical part of the agency's operation, but the employees were very dissatisfied and highly frustrated with the department's startup operation. The project staff for the chief information officer at DHS hired McKinney & Associates to support DHS's enhancement of user support for the information-technology system. The goal was to get all of the employees on the same page. We developed an education program for the employees called *Get IT Right*. Our goal was to help all the workers to understand that, regardless of what agencies they had come from, they must learn and adapt to the new protocols that were established for DHS. A critical linchpin was IT support.

I joined the McKinney team in developing a website, promotional products and training materials to help the new federal agency increase staff awareness of proper IT protocol and technical-support services. One of the most important elements was the development of a brand that the agency and its staff could identify with.

I needed to design the *Get IT Right* brand as an icon that also could be read literally. When you look at the logo, you are able to see and understand the dual message of getting "it" (the new procedures) right and getting "IT" (information technology) right. I used human imagery in the logo to demonstrate that this was a people-oriented program, and its success depended on the people involved. The Department of Homeland Security project team was pleased—and maybe even a little *surprised*—that we were able to meld these two concepts into one simple, effective design.

My Client-Driven Creative Process

I've worked on a wide variety of issues, but there are certain key concepts that I always keep in mind, no matter what the issue. These concepts, honed over the years, have stood me in good stead whether I was working with a large government agency or a small-but-dogged grassroots organization. Let me share them with you.

- *Never let your personal design aesthetic control the process.* I always give the client what I think is right for the situation, but, in the end, they make the final decision. The client is *always* right. Especially when they agree with me.

- *Never take things personally.* Although I treat all of my designs like my children, they still have to go out into the world and fend for themselves. If the client wants to change what I give them based on their own personal or business aesthetic, I can't take it personally.
- *Always ask the client to tell you what they like and don't like in the beginning.* I ask to see examples of what has worked well in the past. Sometimes, a client may have certain guidelines that must be followed. That way, the client's way of thinking becomes clear, and it saves a lot of time and money in the end.
- *Always listen to the client.* This goes along with the previous bullet point, but it's important to emphasize. Get them to give you as much guidance as possible *before* you begin to work.
- *Manage client expectations early.* A lot of times, clients want all of the bells and whistles without fully understanding the whole picture in terms of how the products will be produced. Managing expectations helps the client to hone in on what he or she is really looking for and also makes clear that communications and design cannot solve every problem.

Once I do all these things and have the ingredients I need for a project, then I can say, "Okay, we're going to make a birthday cake" (or, if I have different ingredients, "We're going to make cookies"). Usually, it's what the client already has that inspires the recipe I will use. I normally design with different ideas in mind so that I can give the client a few different versions of the finished product. I want all of my clients to take ownership of the materials I create for them, because it is based on a campaign or issue that they are wholly committed to. In the end, it's always about creating something that achieves its intended purpose and is exactly what they imagined.

These guidelines have been good goal posts for me in all kinds of projects, most recently in campaigns addressing the complex and challenging problem of health inequities in the United States. One of the first of these was the promotion of the PBS series, *Unnatural Causes: Is Inequality Making Us Sick?* Our client, California Newsreel, had already created a logo for the five-part film series, but we wanted to add a special look and feel to it. The newer logo would be a central part of the campaign to promote the films to health-advocacy organizations and grassroots groups around the country. We would use it on press kits and other materials to promote the outreach program. We decided to keep the original logo as a masthead, but to enhance it for the new outreach purpose.

As with the DHS *Get IT Right* campaign, people were an essential component of *Unnatural Causes*, so I wanted to include the human element in its branding. Since we were dealing with health-equity issues across different ethnic groups, I made the imagery slightly muted so that the races of the different individuals couldn't be easily identified. The observer would get the visual impact of men and women of different ethnicities and how they were affected by unnatural causes of chronic illness and death. To reinforce that this film program was about health, I used identifiable medical imagery—such as an EKG reading—to serve as the backdrop to the branding design. I then incorporated the client's original logo over the background that had I created. With this imagery linking the materials, we produced a media kit, complete with a full-color glossy folder and inserts that featured episode highlights, still images and a brochure describing each episode. These materials were widely distributed to the press and the general public to encourage them to watch the TV series and attend film screenings around the country.

With McKinney's continued focus on health equity, I also had the opportunity of working on the *BeWellWomen* campaign, sponsored by the California Department of Public Health. This campaign was aimed at empowering Black women to put their health first.

Before I start my creative process, I like to have all of the necessary background information at hand. *BeWell* was a great project for me because I was presented with up-to-date research on the health of African American women in California, as well as findings from focus groups and polling. The theme of "BE" surfaced from these materials—"Be Well, Be Informed, Be Inspired." I wanted to create a visually exciting logo that would incorporate that theme. The BE logo that I developed incorporated two different typefaces: a heavy, block lettering contrasted by a cursive and stylistic font. Together, these typefaces represented the duality of this campaign: the seriousness of being well and being healthy and also its particular appeal to women. For the color palette, I chose magenta and cyan. I took several things into consideration. I think those colors have feminine qualities, and so I thought they would enhance the focus on women's health. But I was nonetheless concerned, knowing that this campaign would need to show well on various media. This multifaceted campaign incorporated social media, print and video products. We had to consider the best way to effectively communicate the colors without having to worry about color matches. Color is subjective, and the colors can always "change," depending on where you see them. The blue that you see on a computer monitor when looking at a website may not be the same blue that you see printed on a page or the same blue that you see coming out of an office inkjet printer. But when you match the process-printing colors to those of the digital world, you can almost be assured that those colors will register the same way, no matter in what medium they are viewed.

We also learned from the focus groups and polling of the young African American women who would be the target of our campaign that "real" people talking about real-life challenges are the most effective messengers. To accomplish that, we traveled to California to conduct several video shoots, interviewing Black women to speak directly on how they stay healthy. These women became the "faces and voices" of the campaign—a feature that resonated well with our target audience. The client helped select most of the images and material for the campaign. This was a highly collaborative process—something I always encourage.

Roll with the Punches

These were many high points in my career, but I also believe I learn the most from the setbacks and challenges. One of these challenges came in the *BeWellWomen* campaign. In the original conception, we planned to use a complete transit-advertising campaign. I spent hours designing graphics for bus shelters, trains, buses and station billboards—even a short video for the TV monitors on Los Angeles buses. When all of the designs were completed, the California Department of Public Health decided to go in a different direction. After completing about eight separate designs for transit advertising, I needed to switch gears and adapt those designs to appear on church fans, postcards, posters and brochures, which I successfully did.

This project also taught me the importance of flexibility. As the client changed the time for the launch of the campaign, we underwent numerous revisions on themes that required creative revisions, as well, from a Thanksgiving theme ("Be Thankful") to a Yuletide theme ("12 Days of Wellness") to a New Year's theme ("Be Well 24/7 in 2011") theme. Each time, I had to accommodate a new life to the visuals. The lesson here was that everything is subject to change. Sometimes it's not how you prepare for a situation but how you react to the circumstances that you *didn't* prepare for that determines success. When you face difficulty, embrace it! This is how you learn and get better at your craft. I have learned to look beyond personal opinion in order to focus on the interests of the client and the "greater good" of the cause itself.

In some cases, that has meant backing off when I couldn't get a client to see my point of view. In the end, those experiences have helped me become more of a collaborator in the process, which, in turn, makes the client happy with the final product. In the end, a happy client is what all designers should strive for.

At the Table with History Makers

One of the most rewarding aspects of working with McKinney & Associates is meeting extraordinary people who fight for justice on behalf of the voiceless. One of these remarkable people is Elaine Jones, the first woman to serve as director-counsel at the NAACP Legal Defense Fund (LDF). I knew about the great legacy of LDF—its founder and first director-counsel was Thurgood Marshall—and the organization's leadership role in the case of *Brown v. Board of Education*. I felt closer to the institution's tremendous work in social justice, past and present, by working with Elaine Jones, who taught me even more about LDF's outstanding history. It was an honor to assist them with their rebranding projects, and it strengthened my commitment to their work. It has now been years since we've worked together, but it's always a great honor to be acknowledged by her when our paths cross in public.

Lani Guinier was another memorable client of McKinney. When President Clinton nominated her as assistant attorney general, she faced tremendous controversy for some of her courageous writing in support of affirmative action and racial equality. We were able to work with her to fend off attacks from those who wanted to turn the clock back on civil rights. Though the work had very little to do with graphic design, Guinier's stance during this trying time inspired me to be strong and rise above criticism and challenging situations.

For over two decades, my colleagues and friends at McKinney & Associates have sat at the table and joined hands with history makers all over the country and the globe. We have heard them describe their efforts to make this world we live in safer and healthier for everyone, regardless of race, ethnicity, religion, gender or economic status. We have helped them tell their story, and I have helped represent it visually.

When I received my architecture degree in 1981 from Hampton University, I never imagined the impact I would make in the world just by using my passion for visual design and partnering with the right people. I am proud that my work has been part of "public relations with a conscience." Not only has this helped me to give of myself to make a positive impact, it has also given back to me and created a better person.

Musings on Worth

CANDICE FRANCIS

When McKinney & Associates was first contracted to create a multifaceted campaign to raise awareness among African American women in California about preconception health, we knew this effort was going to be very challenging and very rewarding. Our client, the Maternal, Child and Adolescent Health division of the California Department of Public Health, provided us with the most comprehensive research on the health of African American women in today's California—and the information was distressing. Inequality, created by social determinants (poverty, racism, poor housing and low wages) has led to egregious health inequities, with African American women suffering some of the worst outcomes in the state. Infant-mortality rates among African Americans, for example, are more than twice as high as among White Americans.

We knew an effective, engaging and powerful campaign required a firm basis for our belief that the work could and would make a difference for the women we hoped to reach. Our Oakland-based communications consultant, Candice Francis, wrote a short essay that expressed our motivation, our conviction and our aspirations for the campaign. At many points along the way—when we were discouraged by troubling health indicators or missed deadlines—we reread Francis's words and they strengthened our resolve. This is what she wrote:

As I think about the lives of African American women across generations and representative of all socioeconomic levels and educational attainment, it occurs to me that there has been a consistent message directed at us in myriad forms. It is simple yet heinous: Black women are worthless; we lack any real value to this society. We have been defined almost exclusively in deficit terms and cast as victims, our bodies brutalized before we even reached these shores.

I am reminded of my first trip to Africa in the late 1970s. I visited the slave "castle" at Cape Coast in Ghana and witnessed the circular cave where female captives were held at night so that slave traders could stand on a balcony above them and choose who to take for themselves before their load was full and the women were packed like sardines in the decks below.

Upon arrival as slaves, we labored in the fields and homes of our captives while our female nature was conscripted for service at whim. Our children were sold from under us as we nursed White babies so they could grow strong and own us. Countless indignities were borne by our men, whom we could not marry legally. Were they to try to protect us or even show us a modicum of affection, they risked life and limb.

We were depicted as the antithesis of white women. They were pure; we were dirty. They were delicate; we full, big boned and buxom. They were demure; we were brash. They were cherub faced, porcelain skinned with silken hair. We were broad nosed and dark with hair of wool. Indeed, black men would be lynched time and again allegedly because they couldn't control their lust for white women. We were as the writer, Zora Neale Hurston, described in her timeless novel, *Their Eyes Were Watching God*: "de mule uh de world"—and, like a mule, bred to work.

The abolitionist and suffragist Sojourner Truth summarized this painful reality in her famous 1851 speech, "Ain't I a Woman":

Nobody ever helps me into carriages, or over mud-puddles, or gives me any best place! And ain't I a woman? Look at me!

Look at my arm! I have ploughed and planted, and gathered into barns, and no man could head me! And ain't I a woman? I could work as much and eat as much as a man—when I could get it—and bear the lash as well! And ain't I a woman? I have borne thirteen children, and seen most all sold off to slavery, and when I cried out with my mother's grief, none but Jesus heard me! And ain't I a woman?

More than a century later, the movements of the sixties attempted to challenge and reform race, class and gender injustice. Undeniably, gains were made on all fronts, including important milestones for black women. Many of us embraced our unique cultural/racial expression and, coupled with access to education and other valuable commodities, managed to break patterns of poverty and isolation. Yet, while the concepts of "Black Power" and "Black is Beautiful" penetrated the psyche of many African Americans, the parallel universe of the deficit/victim model never disappeared from the mainstream, and our inherent "worthiness" was never inculcated. As the Women's Movement sought parity with (White) men, society was ordered in such a way that they both continued to benefit from the underclass status of Black women. Indeed, the Reagan era would reframe the "mammy" image and charge that "welfare queens"—a.k.a. Black women—were taking advantage of the government's largesse and living "high off the hog" on welfare checks, searing yet another unsympathetic image of black women into the collective consciousness.

"Can we set a tone that speaks to what is at the core of any healthy person—a belief that they can and deserve to be healthy, that they are worthy?"

Fast-forward decades, and Halle Berry becomes the first Black female to win the Oscar for best actress for her portrayal of a desperate woman with an obese son and a husband on death row who finds solace with her husband's White executioner. Nine years later, the best-actress award goes to Sandra Bullock for the true-story depiction of a White woman who saves a Black child's life, while Monique wins best supporting actress for her portrayal as a Black mother who virtually destroys her own daughter. Score 2 for pathology and the deficit/victim model; score 0 for a depiction of worthiness. I offer a simple equation: an image of worthlessness or lack of worthiness defines the portrayal of Black women in the United States. The deficit/victim model is often the launching pad for the story that is told about Black women. No one is holding up an image of Black women as wholesome and valuable and worthy. Surely, we have trailblazers and exceptions too numerous to mention here. A small sample includes Black women who have broken barriers and asserted their "worthiness" despite the deficit/victim model: Oprah Winfrey, Michelle Obama and Gwen McKinney, to name just a few. But among stakeholder groups including policymakers, medical professionals and Black women themselves, too often the appalling reality of statistics is the common denominator for all. How do we engender a sense of worth and value that, over time, could translate into better healthcare—both self-care and policy-care? How do we "flip the script" and tell stories that inspire—like those of African queens (Tiye, Nzinga, Candace, Nehanda, Nefertiti who ruled kingdoms in ancient times—stories that go beyond (or before) slavery, conveying an image of possibility and hope. Can we set a tone that speaks to what is at the core of any healthy person, a belief that they can be, and *deserve* to be, healthy—that they are worthy?

I will leave you with the following lyrics from India Arie. "I Am Not My Hair" considers a subtext that we don't have to be locked in an image or a story; we can shed old belief systems and free ourselves for something new. "I Am Not My Hair" is really about self-worth and value—indispensable ingredients for health.

I am not my hair

I am not this skin

I am not your expectations no no

I am not my hair

I am not this skin

I am a soul that lives within

Street Teams to Sanctuaries:
The Ingredients of Successful
Community Engagement

MICHELE BROWN

McKinney PR Team Conference Call, March, 2011:

"Okay everyone—the schedule for the *BeWellWomen* campaign's final push
has been bumped up. We need to launch the spa sweepstakes a month ahead
of our original schedule. Actually, we need to roll it out in two weeks. We can
do that, can't we?"

This was the confident and by-now-familiar voice of McKinney & Associates'
president, Gwen McKinney. Our favorite taskmaster "Gwen's right hand,
Shawntay" followed up with all the logistical and administrative details.

Meanwhile, in Oakland…

"Sure, Gwen, we can handle it here in northern California."

My mouth said the words, but in my head, I started scrambling. *What in the world?* How were we going to put all this in motion that fast? Well, I thought, reassuring myself, we'd worked other miracles at WordPlay Consulting. We were already becoming known as a company that could produce results quickly; this would have to be no different. The task elements were simple: Pull together a street team to register potential sweepstakes contestants at a Saturday outreach event in a grocery store. Identify and secure the grocery store. Then, for Sunday, find churches that would allow us to convert their regularly scheduled Sunday worship experience into *BeWell Sunday. Hmm. That might not be so easy—even with a substantial donation in hand—but we'll see.* I thought I might rather be Icarus flying to the sun with wax wings than have to talk with some of these pastors with such a small window of opportunity for reflection and decision. But no time for all that; we needed answers, and we needed them quickly.

McKinney & Associates had thoughtfully sprinkled incentives on all of our efforts: for the women who signed up to receive health messages from the *BeWellWomen* campaign, there were grocery gift cards and a chance at winning a fabulous treatment at a local spa; there were wholesale purchases of gift cards for the grocery stores that would let us set up our tables; there was a donation for the churches and there was a decent day's wage for the women who joined the outreach team. For those who do community engagement, incentives are a tool of the trade, and community engagement was at the heart of this stage of the *BeWellWomen* campaign.

The targeted demographic was specific: African American women. The desired outcomes were clear: disseminate an upbeat health and wellness message that would begin to shift negative determinants for health within this group. From our initial focus groups, polling and interviews with women who use the Black Infant Health centers, we already had one vital clue: African American women want to receive health and wellness information from other African American women. This truth informed our outreach efforts in the most fundamental way. My first task was recruiting the street team, and our team members needed to be African American women. Piece o' cake! Or so I thought.

The elements that made this campaign so important were the same ones that made gathering a street team challenging: availability, access and agreement. Who would be available on such short notice to work a full weekend? Did we have good numbers for these busy, distracted, multitasking women, and could we reach them quickly? Since they were busy, distracted, multitasking, working, seeking work, heartbroken, agitated, dating, wishing they were dating, God fearing, churchgoing, single-mothering, elder-caring and working graduate students, would they even be available on such short notice? Well, we were about to see.

That afternoon, I was going to the dog park with Loretta. Her dog, Buster, had recently died, so Gideon—my three-year-old Weimaraner—was her surrogate for now, and we (Gideon and I) were happy to oblige. After 15 minutes of waiting for her at the 7-Eleven on Grand, I got a call from her.

"Girl, my zillerator carburetor master-plug-in rotator fell off! And they *just* put it back on for me. I'll be there in a minute." Huh? What in the world? What is *that*? All I really heard was, "I'll be there in a minute"—when 20 had already passed. By the time our walk was over, though, Loretta was in—some odd combination of boredom, grief and guilt (for making me wait of course) had compelled her to join the effort. I was glad she did; Loretta became my trusted assistant throughout the *BeWellWomen* weekend.

That night on Facebook, I saw that one of my pastor friends was celebrating her daughter's advance to the next grade level of her private school. While publicly rejoicing, she was also privately wondering about how to finance her daughter's extracurricular activities while financing her own seminary training. She also shared that another mutual friend was coming to town the weekend of the project outreach. I hit both of them up on Facebook, and each agreed to help me. Three yeses—I was on a roll! Then, at church, I ran into Jamie, a lovely woman raising her children on her own and launching her own business. Somewhere between the walk around the church to deposit the offering and the handshaking during the benediction, I got her to agree to help us out. One more, and I'd be done.

Mona! Yes! How could I forget her? I thought.

"I've got plans with Damien," she replied, "but let me see what happens."

I counted her in—I knew I would trump plans with a new boyfriend!

The next step was contacting the churches. The faith community can be a challenge when introducing new community programs. Even the term "faith community" had to be further defined by our team. We were not talking about every kind of faith—we were talking specifically about African American Christian churches. Even narrowing down to that has its dichotomies of doctrine and theological worldview. There were three criteria: theologically progressive, community engaged and *large*. If they were at least two of the three, they were eligible. Why were these criteria important? Community-engaged churches understand the importance of the issue of Black women's health, so little explanation would be necessary. Given our short turnaround time to roll out the campaign, we had to engage constituencies that were predisposed to supporting our request and mobilizing on our behalf quickly. Second, we did not have time for any theological battles about women standing in the pulpit, which is also an issue in some churches"thus, progressive churches were selected. Finally, we sought large churches because we wanted to engage the most women possible in the final moments of the campaign with a message of hope, encouragement and community advancement in person and online.

Once the selection criteria were determined, we had to follow the appropriate protocol to reach the people who could make the decisions. In most instances, the pastor has the final say, but advocates for the request are also good for leverage. We were fortunate in this area; I was a member of the clergy and so were several members of our street team. As such, this task became a little easier, since I had relationships with many local pastors. But it also became a little more difficult; some pastors will not tell a stranger no for fear of offense or reprisal, but they can be quick to say someone like me should know better than to ask them to interrupt their regularly scheduled worship programming to make an announcement and solicitation. The *BeWellWomen* campaign wanted to get commitments from mega churches—congregations of 1,000 or more—but I know these are the most difficult to engage on short notice. In the end, we compromised: I targeted medium-to-large congregations that were community conscious and flexible (meaning that they understood these kinds of public-education opportunities and appreciated the donation attached). Plus, no matter how I sliced it, it would be a favor to *me*—so the question became, "Who can do me a solid?"

Rev. Dr. Charley Hames, Jr., pastor of Beebe Memorial Cathedral in Oakland, is my friend and colleague"a young, politically astute and community-conscious clergyman with a penchant for innovative programming. I knew he would do this for me. I Facebooked him the request and the details; he passed these on to a member of his staff, and after a 15-minute conversation, it was done. She's a mother of two teenagers and knows the stress of a high-powered, two-career family (her husband is a partner in a big accounting firm). She could relate to the need to share relevant health-and-wellness information, and she could attest to the inherent stress found even in what anyone would call a good life. As I explained the *BeWell* campaign, she interjected.

"Michele, I had the best doctors, insurance and medical care, and I was still on three months of bed rest because my work was so stressful. I broke out in a rash; I had preeclampsia—unnecessary complications. My husband was so worried. The last pregnancy really taught me about the value of self-care and what real wellness looks like. This *BeWell* campaign is much needed in our community and in the church."

By the end of our conversation, my team had a table, microphone time on the program and permission to engage the women as they entered and departed the sanctuary. This discussion of health and wellness for African American women was really resonating with people. One down, two more to go!

Bishop Keith Clark is one of the most cutting-edge, community-minded pastors in Oakland and a dear friend. I call him "the people's pastor." He's very close to the community and is a beloved leader. He readily agreed to let me come to his church. That invitation gave us access to the bulls-eye of our demographic: working-class and middle-income African American women of childbearing age who were too busy for good nutrition and too distracted for self-care, but who would be deeply appreciative of these things if given.

The pastor of Lily of the Valley Christian Center, the third church I contacted, gave me an immediate call back. This church was the smallest of the three but was located in an area that not only needed this kind of information but was crippled by the lack thereof. Bishop Willis, the pastor, asked me for more details about the campaign.

"The *BeWell* campaign," I told him, "is targeting African American women of childbearing age, because we are more likely not to carry to full term.

As a matter of fact, we consistently, no matter what our socioeconomic status, deliver babies too small and too soon, and usually it is because of stress. Our White counterparts do not have this issue. We have some of the worst prenatal health and birth outcomes of any other ethnic group in California."

"Well, by all means, come share with us," Bishop Willis responded. "We have so many young women of childbearing age in our church; this would be a blessing and an encouragement to them—and that spa package really sweetens the deal."

I thanked him and told him I'd see him Sunday.

Last-Minute Wrinkles

The week of the outreach, I realized that I had a few more contacts to make. I needed to reach out to the Black Infant Health agencies we'd been working with. The staff there was excited about the campaign and enthusiastic about signing up their clients for the spa sweepstakes. I also had to touch base with the day spa that would be providing the services for the sweepstakes. The spa owner and I worked out a way to reach their guests with the information without disrupting a peaceful, refreshing experience. She also agreed to display information about the campaign in her window—which was great, since they faced a parking lot in a busy mall.

Because life happens and unforeseen events occur, a couple of my street-team members had to pull out. It worked out just fine but reminded me that I should always have a contingency list of people who can fill in. Fortunately, team was so motivated that there was no need for replacements.

Food

Small gestures go a long way when you're working with a street team. At our planning meeting, I asked my friend, a gourmet chef, to whip up something lovely for the women. Good food is a great inspiration. Some people who told me they couldn't attend the meeting changed their answer when I told them my friend Chef Reign was preparing dinner for us.

That evening, we reviewed all the event details. Team members came up with some great approaches for the grocery-store outreach—everything from, "Hey, for five minutes of your time, I can save you five dollars on your grocery bill!" to "If you give me a few minutes, you could win a trip to the spa!" to "Could you use a break? I've got one if you've got a minute." Beyond us pitching the approach, we had a genuine dialogue about what it means to "be well." We talked about self-care and its complexity. What did wellness really mean to us as African American women? Sherice began.

"I'm so stressed, if I went on a week's vacation, it would take me four days just to settle down and unwind to *enjoy* a vacation. It would be closer to detox!"

Another street team member commented.

"Girl, I'm on the go so much, when I sit still, I tip right over—asleep. My daughter usually just covers me up, and I wake up in the wee hours of the morning in my work clothes. I change for bed with only a few hours left before I'm back on the same hamster wheel again."

"Did you know that stress is the number-one cause of preterm births and poor birth outcomes among African American women, no matter *what* their socioeconomic status?" I chimed in. Andrea responded, "Yep, we've got to slow down—the success of our families depends on it. I was sick because I couldn't forgive my father. Girl, when I finally did, not only did I feel better, but I dropped the physical weight that had attached itself to me as a result."

"Hmm, I know the feeling," said another street-team member. "But what to do in the meantime?"

"Breathe through the contractions, girl!" I used that pregnancy metaphor having never been pregnant but having been in protracted seasons of pain. "You get the picture right?" Collectively they answered, "Yeah, girl!"

We all laughed over a plate of Chef Reign's now-infamous white lasagna with Alfredo sauce, broccoli florets, smoked chicken and shrimp. The street team loved it, and the food was almost as good as the conversation.

Game Day is...when execution is crucial and there is no room for error—everything has to unfold as it should.

Game Day

"Game Day" is the term most event planners use to describe the strike-zone timeline of the event. It's when execution is crucial and there is no room for error—everything has to unfold as it should. Game Day can be the week of, the days before or the day of the event. On this Game Day, I was awakened by the alarm clock and the weather forecast.

"Good morning, Bay Area! Today is gonna be the soggiest day of the season—torrential rain showers will blanket the area for the most of the day. If I were you, I would stay in and bundle up; it's gonna be a messy one."

The weatherman was already trying to kill my joy! I had a 10-hour day ahead of me and I needed to do it in a raincoat and rubber boots? And what of my street team?

Well, here goes, I thought. First, I dropped the dog off at daycare; I couldn't concern myself with his care, feeding and bladder maintenance for the day. Then it was off to pick up the tables and chairs we'd use to table at the grocery store. Of course, traffic was gnarly, and I was already getting a spate of texts from my street team telling me they were going to be late. The newscaster had been right: this was a morning to not even open the blinds; it was *that* gray and uninviting. The news was filled with reports of flash flooding and ground saturation. I'd never even heard of such a thing—that the ground could not hold any more water. "Stiff upper lip, girl—call upon your British roots! You've gotta make this work," I reminded myself. When the traffic finally subsided, I was 15 minutes late, too, but thankfully two of my team members were already at the grocery story and ready to go.

My teammates set up quickly, and we were off to the races—until I saw that there was another organization setting up at the entrance I thought we'd use. I was baffled. The store manager, Maurice, had never mentioned that there would be anyone else there. I definitely needed to talk to him,

was a wise and effective strategy to infuse the worship experience with the *BeWell* campaign message. *BeWell Sunday* was a smashing success.

Postgame Wrap-Up

At the end of the weekend, I paid everyone and took Loretta to dinner on Sunday; she'd been with me as an assistant, and it was the least I could do. I delivered the donation checks to the churches on Monday and received thank-you letters in return. *BeWell Sunday* was very well received. Women *still* stop me to tell me how much they enjoyed my remarks. Everyone loved the church fans, and, of course, who couldn't use 500 dollars in this economy? I've since visited these churches and seen the fans in rotation, and our flyers still lay out as informational resources.

Black women, as Alice Walker declared decades ago, are universal beasts of burden—we cannot be so any longer. Our lives, the lives of our children and the vitality of our communities depend on us being healthy and whole, not halfway heaven-bound. Self-care is not selfish; it is key to our survival.

Now it's Monday afternoon, and *BeWell Weekend* is finally over. I need a manicure, pedicure (my feet could cut diamonds!) and a nap. The phone's ringing— it's Gwen!

"So, tell us: how did the *BeWell Weekend* go in Oakland?"

Tortured Trail to Triumph

You don't meet a Susan Burton every day. Along the tortured trail of abuse and tragedy, she has cleared extraordinary hurdles, landing on solid ground to teach and inspire criminal justice reform through her personal triumph and public example.

Susan Burton, one of six siblings and the only girl, never had the luxury of being "the precious princess." The jagged edges of those formative years taught Susan to become who she is today. Caretaker. Fighter. Survivor. Six-time prison inmate. Serial rape victim. Substance abuser. A daughter of the streets, she could scoop up the despair in the air and breathe it as her oxygen.

Susan's story and the message of A New Way of Life Reentry Project that she founded in 1998 is a clarion call for reentry. It nurtures redemption and advances reform. It is a lesson of forgiveness for individual acts of abuse and peels away the layers to systemic injustice that reduces people into broken war casualties. The victims lack access to a different pathway, forced to rely on their own fragile

Get short, timely messages from Susan Burton.
Twitter is a rich source of instantly updated information. It's easy to stay updated on an incredibly wide variety of topics. Join today and follow @Susan4CNNHero

Sign Up ›

Susan4CNNHero

The @LATimes features Susan & her New Way of Life charity in story on LA charities seeking help for the holidays. http://lat.ms/hunGuu

Social Media and Social Justice: Reach and Impact

PAMELA TAYLOR AND TAMARA BRAUNSTEIN

Since 1990, when Gwen McKinney embarked on the journey of practicing "Public Relations with a Conscience," communications and public-education campaigns have evolved into multimedia, multi-sensory labyrinths designed to reach the largest possible audience with the greatest possible impact. Of course, the twin goals of reach and impact have always been key to the firm's social justice campaigns. From amplifying the voices of public servants and frontline workers to lifting the covers off the indignities against people worldwide, the firm's campaigns have harnessed the arsenal of communications and media tools to raise public awareness and right societal wrongs. Fast-forward to today's world of Internet, e-mail, Google, Facebook, Twitter and YouTube; what is the interplay between social media and social justice? In a conversation between veteran communications pro, Pamela Taylor, and emerging PR practitioner, Tamara Braunstein, we explore this subject.

PT: Why social networking?

TB: It's here, and it's *now*. It's instant. It's versatile. It works. My generation was raised in a culture of "give it to me now," and there's really no turning back. Progress—in all its shapes and forms—is constant, and social media are a natural fit in our consumption-based, progress-driven society. That can be taken for better or for worse, but, for the most part, I believe it to be for the better. There are some who still balk at social networking, decrying it as disguised narcissism, but that's such a limited view.

PT: How would you say this instantaneous and virtual space is beneficial?

TB: I think the majority of us who have adopted social networking into our daily and professional lives have witnessed, on some level, its power as a tool to really connect us to things and people we care about. We're living in a world where messaging is literally instant. And it's powerful. In this day and age, a member of Congress can be forced to resign because of his inappropriate tweeting habits. A virtual nobody in a foreign town can become an overnight sensation because he decides to tweet about helicopter activity outside his window. I can't think of a more adaptable and accessible communication tool. At this point, the possibilities really *are* endless.

PT: How might it have made a difference in McKinney's early campaigns?

TB: Social media present so many new opportunities for positive growth; at a place like McKinney, that's invaluable. Looking back through the firm's portfolio, it's quite intriguing to think, "Wow, if they could do all that back then, imagine what they could do today." To me, one of the most moving stories in this book is about Leila McDowell's fight against how the Fairfax, Virginia, education system treated her autistic daughter. Granted, awareness for autism has dramatically increased in recent years, but the advent of social media played (and plays) a huge role in its continued rise as a hot issue. In her essay, Leila talks about how she successfully organized a demonstration outside of her daughter's school to draw awareness to the controversy. There's not a doubt in my mind that with social networking as a resource, the "frantic reaction" that demonstration earned would have stretched far beyond the boundaries of Fairfax and the metro area.

PT: Does social networking change the impact of traditional media?

TB: Yes and no. At least, I would say, it doesn't take away from the value of traditional media and other tried-and-tested communications tactics. As I said before, there are those who still shy away from social media, whatever their reasons. It's not so much a matter of generational divide either; my mother's age group dominates Facebook now. It even took me a while to warm up to the idea of Twitter, and I was a journalist.

People adjust to new technology at their own pace, and some will always prefer to sit down and turn the pages of the Sunday paper instead of pushing a button on their e-reader. Social media and traditional media are not interchangeable, nor are they mutually exclusive. In fact, I'd say the most successful organizations know how to effectively pair old and new. Digital and traditional platforms reach different groups of people.

PT: So, from your perspective, what's the difference in impact?

TB: It's not necessarily that one affects the impact of another; it's more that each impacts a group uniquely. Attention span is the biggest difference. When I'm online, I will browse a page for a few seconds, and if it doesn't hold my attention, I move on. If I buy a newspaper though, I've already made a conscious decision that I want to read it. In the PR world, it's sort of the same thing. Just because you announce something online doesn't mean you can depend on it to be seen or heard. As quickly as I can post an update, that same update will no doubt be pushed down in the feeds of my followers as the rest of their networks broadcast their news. Social media is really just a stellar way to amplify what you're already doing via traditional practice.

PT: Since being with McKinney, how has it changed your perspective (if at all) on the use and impact of social media on social-justice campaigns?

TB: It's changed my perspective dramatically. Before I knew that people and organizations employed social media as tools for their campaigns, I never thought about the strategy behind it. I followed several groups of interest to me on Twitter, and I "liked" a few Facebook pages, but the fact that my actions affected their measurements of how they engage their audiences was a revelation. Whatever apprehensions I had against directly communicating with a campaign basically disintegrated. I started to view my networks less as a necessary evil and more as my go-to resources.

It's really amazing how much people know and how eager they are to share that knowledge. Social media allows campaigns—especially social-justice campaigns—to tap into that desire and transform apathy to action. My work with McKinney on the campaign to move Walmart to sign a community-benefits agreement with the citizens of DC was truly eye opening in that manner. When our client came to us, it was general knowledge that Walmart wanted to open four stores in the District, and all at once. It was by and large accepted as a done deal. Through actively engaging constituents and media—including traditional media of print and broadcast—via social media, we were able to really influence the dialogue around the issue, transforming it from an economic issue to a social-justice concern.

PT: We always learn from each new experience. What was your takeaway from that campaign?

TB: It taught me that navigating social media is an art, and learning to craft your message based on the platform you choose is just as important as determining why you're doing it in the first place.

Managing a Train Wreck: When the Red Line Derailed

JACKIE JETER

In the history of modern train wrecks, the Metrorail crash on June 22, 2009, ranks among the deadliest. Nine people were killed and some 80 others were injured when a train packed with evening-rush-hour commuters plowed into a stopped train on the Washington Metro system's busiest rail service. The train operator, Jeanice McMillan, a member of ATU Local 689 and the mother of a college freshman, was among the fatalities.

The collision catapulted the Washington Metropolitan Area Transit Authority (WMATA) into a crisis. Everyone clamored for answers—the workers, the riding public, federal and local government officials and the media. As for me, I needed to be in touch with my constituency—the more than 7,500 Metro workers who operate the nation's second-largest rail-transit system. If ever a crisis communications plan was needed, June 22 was the day.

Little did I know that Monday would be like no other. It was early summer, and the sun shimmered across the DC sky. I remember feeling that something was in the air. Unease nagged at me all day. And then, shortly after 5:02 that evening, the phones in the union hall started ringing madly, delivering the tragic news. With a sense of urgency, my fellow officers and I rushed to the site. My husband, Roland Jeter, first vice president of ATU Local 689, and I arrived to the crash scene, on the Red Line, between the Fort Totten and Takoma Metro stations at the New Hampshire Avenue overpass. (Ft. Totten and Takoma are border neighborhoods between DC and Silver Spring, Maryland.) It was still rush hour. A dense crowd of spectators had gathered and was separated by yellow strips of police barricades. Roland and I worked our way to the edge of the fenced-in perimeter to take stock of the devastation. Rubble and remnants of smoldering steel were piled among the charred debris. The acrid smell of death and catastrophe filled the air.

Amid a legion of somber faces, I saw Metro general manager John Cato. Our eyes locked in mournful disbelief. How could this have happened? The crash defied everything I had been taught in my years working this system as a Metrorail operator and rail-traffic controller. Under a pall of raw sadness, Cato and I walked toward one another and embraced. The often-opposing sides we occupy—management versus workers—didn't matter at that point—a Metro worker and eight passengers had perished on our watch. My first priority was to try to piece together the scattered shards of truth in the remains of the wreckage.

The unforeseen tragedy catapulted Metro into living rooms, offices and the Internet by news cameras trained on the crash site. WMATA scrambled to get a message out in the first news cycle. General Manager Cato's public statement was plain and strategic: "The system is safe."

Safe. Really? I heard the not-so-disguised message behind his simple words. If the system was safe, then the operator must have done something wrong; so commenced the blame game. My members, already in mourning and feeling vulnerable, did not deserve that response from Metro. In those critical first moments, I had thought that Cato and I shared an understanding. I had thought we shared a joint goal of making sure this kind of tragedy would never happen again to workers and riders. But in Cato's media statements, I recognized the nuance of finger pointing and immediately saw it for what it was: a stealth attempt to scapegoat train operator Jeanice McMillan. I wasn't having it. Nor was my public-relations firm, McKinney & Associates.

McKinney's value was tested like never before in the hours and days that followed the Red Line disaster.

Crisis Communications

Shortly after I was elected to my first three-year term as president of ATU Local 689 in December 2007, Joslyn Williams, president of the AFL-CIO Washington Metropolitan Council and mentor to me, suggested that I engage a strategic-communications partner to help define and amplify the union's voice. He recommended McKinney & Associates because of the firm's stellar history of helping unions and other social-justice organizations drive change on important social issues, including workers' rights. Joslyn, who had been among the firm's earliest clients, proved to be a prescient counselor, and McKinney's value was tested like never before in the hours and days that followed the Red Line disaster.

McKinney immediately developed and rolled out a muscular crisis-communications plan that focused on hammering out a clear message for our union. They also established clear and sustained lines of communications to a diverse audience of Local 689 stakeholders. We identified these as our union members, the riding public, WMATA, local elected officials, the National Transportation Safety Board (NTSB) and federal and local transportation policymakers.

In the immediate aftermath of the catastrophic crash, the media clatter was incessant. Events seemed to be running into each other with public questions and members' anxiety colliding in freefall. In the course of four days, we convened four news conferences. The stakes were high; we had to be strong and nimble. This was where the expertise of McKinney & Associates took the foreground. The firm's full-throttle crisis-communication plan included these critical activities:

Defining the issue and immediately occupying clear and uncontested ground in the public debate. Developing a message framework for shaping all written and verbal communications;

- *Rapidly creating press statements, news releases, media advisories and commentary capturing our voice and the moment;*
- *Following breaking crash findings issued by NTSB;*
- *Maintaining vigilant contact and engagement with reporters and editors covering the story;*
- *Monitoring the public statements of WMATA for the union's reaction and rebuttal;*
- *Tracking news coverage to measure the reach and impact of the union's messaging and outreach;*
- *Guaranteeing accessibility from dawn to midnight.*

The Personal Side of a National Tragedy

McKinney & Associates took the extra step: they were always there for me personally. They had my back. Admittedly, I often have to be prodded to step up to the microphone or camera. Intellectually, I understand the importance of gaining public light on behalf of my members and our issues. But to this day, I'd rather be low-key and out of the spotlight. McKinney intuitively understood that the voice of the union was a crucial part of the strategy to illuminate the safety problems of WMATA. They ensured that the media had constant access to me. As invasive as it felt, I also understood that this was not about my comfort or desire for privacy; the weight of my members and our fallen comrade rested on my shoulders. Leadership meant sounding my voice—not just for me or for the union officers, but for our members who needed to know that Jeanice McMillan would not be twice a victim, by foul play and scapegoating, even before she was laid to rest.

In the lifecycle of public tragedies, funerals assume a tremendous space, providing an opportunity for closure and reflection in the loss for those most aggrieved. Though there is an element of voyeurism, the public event more importantly enables us to put a period on the end of a tragic sentence. I deployed Gwen McKinney and her team to work with the McMillan family, and they were able to transform themselves from publicists in rapid-fire engagement with the media to compassionate aides of the bereaved. Thrust into the public spotlight at a time of utter sadness, Jeanice's family members needed a buffer and support to field media queries and assist them in managing the cameras and reporters who descended on the homes of relatives and on the funeral service. Managing those elements required an understanding of the protocols of passage. My trust in the firm was not betrayed. The contribution from McKinney was vital and specific, even helping the family prepare Jeanice's obituary.

From Scapegoat to Hero

In the wake of the tragedy, transit workers were tense and up in arms. For years, WMATA has operated within a culture of blaming workers for break-downs in safety while ignoring the very real threats to the men and women who wore the Metro uniform. Metrobus operators have been spat on, have had objects and fluid thrown at them, have had knives and guns pointed at them and have been sexually assaulted. Despite the union's urging to beef up the presence of Metro police officers on troubled bus routes and to fix broken security cameras, attacks on Metrobus operators continue to occur unabated without adequate protection from WMATA.

WMATA's penchant for scapegoating workers drove public speculation that perhaps Jeanice had been texting or talking on her cell phone at the time of the crash, and my members were furious that Metro would suggest that scenario without any basis in fact. As the first forensic threads of the crash emerged, the NTSB debunked the careless innuendo with evidence that Jeanice's cell phone was located at the crash site, tucked away in her backpack. With McKinney's support, I moved swiftly to get the message out that Jeanice was in no way responsible for the collision. I coupled the defense of Jeanice with a sustained barrage of questions about the "fail-safe" computer system that was supposed to be smarter than human calculation, equipment malfunctions, the need to put the trains on manual operations and other management questions that the WMATA officials would not answer.

Jeanice McMillan was a hero, and McKinney helped us amplify that message.

The firm's intensive outreach won media trust and public engagement. The outcome was transformative: Jeanice McMillan was recast from a scapegoat to hero. The union's demand for drastic and immediate safety measures began to dominate the conversation about the crash. The messaging crafted by McKinney amplified the ultimate sacrifice Jeanice had made to protect the safety of riders; she had courageously stayed the course as the train careened toward certain calamity, bravely applying the break and maintaining her position at the helm of the train. The skilled train operator, union member and mother could have easily abandoned her post and hunkered down for protection. Instead, she put the lives of her passengers before her own.

Jeanice McMillan was a hero, and McKinney helped us amplify that message. McKinney's strategy also transformed the union's relationship with the media; from nemesis and inquisitor, the press instead became watchdog and partner in our push to get answers and expose the dangers of the system. In the ensuing months, McKinney drew on every preliminary NTSB report that linked the accident to equipment error and used the authoritative NTSB findings as content for updated press statements. The firm's vigilance supported our ongoing effort to demand immediate and lasting emphasis on improving safety. Through McKinney's push to keep the union's voice in the debate, the media continued to shine a light of scrutiny on WMATA's safety deficiencies.

The June 22 crash shattered our sense of safety. More than a year after that fateful crash, NTSB released its final report, citing "equipment error" as the cause of the accident.

Metro workers are vital to the region's economy, lifestyle and vibrancy; they make it possible for millions of commuters to get to and from work and for millions of visitors to travel across the region with ease. On weekdays, Metro transports an average of 1.2 million riders by rail and bus. The train crash on June 22 was on the Red Line, whose stations traverse from northern Virginia through the heart of DC to the outer reaches of suburban Maryland. Weekend ridership on the system averages nearly 300,000 people. Public transportation in our sprawling metropolis is as vital as water, electricity and other public utilities. As soaring gas prices continue to impose pain at the pumps, public-transit workers are essential to the region's economy, the environment and the general quality of life.

But this vital lifeline has still not repaired itself. For safety reasons, Metrorail went to manual operation after the catastrophic June 22, 2009, accident, and has still not returned to automatic operations. Years later, the automatic-braking system remains susceptible to a single-point failure that could result in another disaster of equal or greater magnitude. Each day, the men and women of Metro go to work with the expectation of returning home to their loved ones. That's not an excessive expectation for any worker—or passenger. That is why we will continue to speak out and to keep our union voice strong; we learned just how important that is during the crisis of the Red Line train wreck. McKinney's strategic communications counsel and services in those critical hours helped assure my union's voice was heard and our fallen co-worker remembered as the hero she proved to be.

A four-hour documentary series exploring our socio-economic and racial inequities in health

Airing four consecutive Thursdays, March 27 to April 17, 2008 (check local listings)

PBS

UNNATURAL CAUSES
...is inequality making us sick?

A CONVERSATION WITH LARRY ADELMAN & LLEW SMITH

Series Creator/Executive Producer Larry Adelman and Co-Executive Producer Llew Smith offer insights on the art, the science and the inspiration behind their new series.

What inspired UNNATURAL CAUSES? Where did the process begin and where did it take you?

Larry Adelman: The seed was planted several years ago when we were making RACE - The Power of an Illusion, a series that explored popular myths and misconceptions about race. We found out that African Americans have one of the highest hypertension rates in the world. The knee-jerk hypothesis among some scientists was that this had something to do with genes, but that idea was exploded by research showing that West Africans (whose ancestors are shared by many African Americans) enjoy one of the lowest hypertension rates in the world. Instead of some mythical genetic variant, the real culprit behind these high blood pressure rates is more likely rooted in the stresses of everyday life particular to the African American experience, i.e., racism. That's when we first realized how the "outside" – our social and economic environment – could get under our skin and disrupt our biology as surely as germs and viruses.

As the RACE series screened around the country, folks brought to our attention literally hundreds of studies and journal articles describing the many pathways by which class and racism influence health outcomes as surely as diet, smoking and exercise do. And we learned that it isn't just African Americans or the poor leading sicker, shorter lives because of inequality, but white, middle class Americans too.

Llew Smith: This series led us to go further than exploding myths. The journey of *UNNATURAL CAUSES* took us to deconstructing our very ideas about health in society. Many believe that being healthy is as simple as making smart choices: exercising, eating well, taking a vacation every so often to reduce stress, having networks to support us and so on. But behaviors explain only part of the story. When we

Larry Adelman & Llew Smith

(continued on page 2)

unnaturalcauses.org   Produced by California Newsreel with Vital Pictures • Presented by the National Minority Consortia of public television

CALIFORNIA NEWSREEL

Vital PICTURES

NMC NATIONAL MINORITY CONSORTIA

Unnatural Causes: Changing the Way Americans Think about Health

LARRY ADELMAN

It often appears as though Americans are obsessed with health and fitness. Scan the magazine section at any supermarket or airport in the country, and you'll encounter dozens of cover headlines like this: "Ten Foods to Eat to Live to 100," "Five Ways to Protect Your Heart" and "Three Simple Steps to Reduce Stress." We spend more than twice per person on medical care than the average rich country, and one in every four Americans aged 45 to 64 took three or more prescription drugs last month.

What you're *unlikely* to spot are many headlines like this: "Living Wage Jobs Bring Health Benefits" or "Affordable Housing Linked to Healthy Hearts & Arteries." Or anything about how universal preschool, desegregation, better transit and other *social policies* can improve our health by improving our lives. Which is odd, since the evidence is overwhelming—documented in hundreds of studies and journal articles—that the economic and social conditions in which we are born, live, work, play and age can actually get under our skin, change our physiology and affect our health as surely as germs and viruses. As Harvard public-health professor Nancy Krieger says, "Our history is written into our bodies." Our bodies reflect an accumulation of conditions that start in childhood and, in the words of Jack Shonkoff, director of the National Center on the Developing Child, can lead to "a cascade of advantage for some, a pileup of risk for others."

Yet despite all the evidence, this *story* of how economic and social forces shape our health has been all but absent from mainstream media. Public policy, popular opinion and journalism have been stuck in the conventional biomedical narrative that focuses almost exclusively on what individuals can do to be healthy. And so we set out to produce what would become *Unnatural Causes: Is Inequality Making Us Sick?* a four-hour documentary series, broadcast by PBS in spring 2008 that explored the root causes of our alarming class and racial inequities in health. We didn't simply want to document unequal outcomes but rather render visible what drives those outcomes and, in doing so, tell a new story about how societal conditions and political decisions can make us healthy—or sick.

The United States has among the worst health and shortest life expectancies of any industrialized nation—and the greatest health inequalities.

How does one challenge a deeply imprinted discourse or way of thinking? We began our work even before we drafted film outlines, by convening an advisory team of brilliant scholars, public health officials, advocates, representatives of community-based organizations and McKinney & Associates to review the research and consider how such a documentary series might effectively reframe the way Americans look at health. We knew that communications could not be a substitute for a social movement built around health equity, but a powerful communications agenda could call into question many of the assumptions that the public and policymakers take for granted about the root causes of health and wellness and, in so doing, enlarge the public space, lay the groundwork and perhaps even feed an eagerness for new ideas grounded in what scholars call the social determinants of health equity.

The Conventional Narrative

The United States has among the worst health and shortest life expectancies of any industrialized nation—and the greatest health inequalities. And it's not just the poor who are sick; even middle-class White folks will die, on average, almost three years sooner than the rich. And at every stop on the economic pyramid, African Americans, Native Americans, and Pacific Islanders, on average, fare worse than their white counterparts. Awareness has been growing about this stark inequality, yet these findings are commonly rationalized away; they don't "stick." Research commissioned by the Robert Wood Johnson Foundation revealed that unequal outcomes are commonly thought of as "unfortunate but not necessarily unfair." One reason, our advisors argued, is because the public holds in its head an individual, biomedical model of health that serves as the "common sense" prism through which it filters, interprets and gives meaning to health news and blinds itself to the social determinants of health inequities. We identified five basic components of this conventional biomedical model. No health-equity communications strategy could succeed, we felt, unless it could eventually rupture this discourse and begin to suture together a new one.

- *Health is conflated with health care. The battles over health insurance, plus the barrage of ads for drugs ("Ask your doctor") and new medical technologies continually reinforce the importance of health care. Yet that unequal access to health care—as shameful as it is—results in no more than 10 to 20 percent of the differences in population health outcomes.*
- *Personal responsibility and right choices. Prevention has become equated with persuading Americans to make healthy choices such as eating right, exercising and avoiding tobacco and narcotics. As a result, most Americans— and policymakers—assume that unequal population health outcomes are the consequence of individuals making the wrong choices, be it from ignorance, lack of self-discipline, cultural practices or "lifestyles." This framework removes individuals from their societal context, reinforces the divide between "them" and "us" and stops political action dead in its tracks.*
- *Health gaps are unfortunate but not necessarily unfair. While progressives tend to view unequal population outcomes as evidence of injustice, for most Americans, hierarchy simply reinforces their view that the world is working as it should, reflecting choices made by self-determining individuals. If some groups fare worse than others, that's simply more evidence they made the wrong choices, have a dysfunctional culture or even have bad genes.*

- *Technology as a deus ex machina. Medical advances (especially drugs and, eventually, stem-cell and genomic breakthroughs) constitute the magic that will eventually bring us all a long and healthy life.*
- *Nothing can be done. Racial and class health gaps (when acknowledged) are viewed as deeply entrenched and too big a problem to address. This resignation, even cynicism, feeds on a distrust of government. And when those different health outcomes are perceived as the logical result of personal behaviors, government interventions are easily disparaged as the "behavioral police" or the "nanny state."*

Where we are born, live, work and play have a greater impact on our chances to live healthy lives than even smoking

A New Story

The exciting news is that the scientific evidence is now very clear that where we are born, live, work and play have a greater impact on our chances to live healthy lives than even smoking. But if *Unnatural Causes* were to succeed in directing the public's attention to these social determinants of health equity, it would have to incorporate the evidence into a new *story*, one capable of displacing the conventional individual, biomedical narrative. We took our cue from a statement by the World Health Organization (WHO): "Evidence is rarely, if ever, sufficient by itself to catalyze political action. In political terms, what might be at least as crucial as the evidence itself is the 'story' in which it is embedded." We needed to come up with a way to tell a good story that illustrated not just unequal outcomes but the "upstream" inequities that drive those outcomes.

Health equity is a new idea for most people. It's not difficult to grasp, but it does require us to change the way we present stories about health differences. Health equity is *not* about different outcomes, per se. Disparities or inequalities in health arise from many factors, including plain darn luck. Health *equity* concerns those differences in population health that are systemic, socially produced and preventable—and thus inherently unjust and unfair.

In other words, health equity is about those outcomes that can be traced to inequities in other arenas of our lives: the jobs we do, the wages and benefits they pay, neighborhood conditions, the quality of our schools, the power we have to manage the conditions that impinge upon our lives and so on. These are every bit as much health issues as are diet, tobacco and exercise. Because power and societal resources are distributed unequally by class and by race, so, too, are our patterns of health and disease. In its final report, "Closing the Gap in a Generation," the WHO Commission on Social Determinants of Health puts it this way: "The unequal distribution of health-damaging experiences is not a 'natural' phenomenon but is the result of a toxic combination of poor social policies and programs, unfair economic arrangements and bad politics." McKinney & Associates helped us to identify six key elements that would illuminate this story.

1. Focus on the Social Determinants of Health Equity

It's not enough to demonstrate unequal outcomes. Even when the media *do* run an occasional story about health "disparities" (i.e., different outcomes), much of the public is still likely to blame the victim for making the wrong choices. We needed to refocus our lens on the inequitable social structures, institutions and social and economic arrangements that generate and drive those outcomes.

There are two parts to helping people recognize this. First, we should certainly acknowledge that behaviors and individual responsibility are important, but we also need to demonstrate how *the behavioral choices we make are often constrained by the choices we have*: the challenges of getting five to seven servings of fruits and vegetables a day while living in a food desert or of shopping and cooking after a long commute or working two jobs; the difficulty of exercising if the neighborhood isn't safe and walkable and lacks parks and green space; or, perhaps even more commonly, if long working hours and commutes and lack of child care preclude the time to exercise, shop and cook. Environments also shape social norms that, in turn, influence behaviors.

But we felt it equally essential to demonstrate how many health outcomes have *nothing* to do with individual choice whatsoever: the location of toxic dumps, the quality of schools, whether factories stay open or shift jobs overseas, where parks and freeways—or public transit—get built, the wages and benefits jobs pay, regulation of the mortgage market and foreclosures, even tax policy; these are all examples of government and corporate decisions over which individuals have little say and which can expose us to health threats or health promoters. These all profoundly affect our opportunities to live healthy and flourishing lives and, because these societal resources are distributed unequally by class and by race, so, too, are our patterns of health and disease.

2. Redefine Risky Behaviors

We know that smoking, drinking, lack of exercise and fast food diets are all risky behaviors. But what about the behavior of bankers who issued predatory loans and in their wake left block after block empty and millions of lives destroyed? Or the bond traders whose securitized derivatives and collateralized debt swaps made those predatory loans not only possible but profitable—and brought our economy down while doing so? Or the lobbyists for agribusiness and the food industry and their paid pawns in Congress who subsidize corn—and thus corn syrup and obesity—with our tax dollars? Or General Motors executives who spent millions opposing seat belts and other safety regulations—and then mileage standards—and whose refusal to invest their profits in new, fuel-efficient automotive technologies finally led to bankruptcy and the loss of tens of thousands of jobs? Or those corporations that have dumped their pensions entirely or the many others that cost-shifted pension risk onto the backs of employees by selling Americans on the magical virtues of 401(k) plans so that now retirees find their material assets unexpectedly slashed, their futures uncertain and their health at risk?

Couldn't we redefine these actions as risky behaviors and assess them not only in the currency of profitability but also in the currency of health?

3. Redefine Compliance: Hold Government and Corporations as Well as Individuals Accountable

This is a corollary to redefining risky behaviors. Doctors hold patients responsible for taking their medications. If they don't take them, they're labeled noncompliant. But what about a poor asthma patient who lives in a damp and moldy apartment overrun with cockroaches and vermin and is constantly exposed to asthma triggers? Why couldn't we hold her landlord to be out of compliance, as well—or the housing department or the mayor charged with enforcing housing laws and regulations? Or the legislators who write the laws? Or, most of all, the political and legal arrangements that allow large developers, their trade associations, lobbyists, publicists and media campaigns to exercise such one-sided, disproportionate power over government officials and their decisions that lead to the inequities and oppression faced by our asthma patient?

Since the conditions for health are created by the individual, by government and by corporate decisions, shouldn't we hold *each* accountable? Elected officials can make policies that influence the kinds of jobs available, whether they are secure or will move overseas, the money and benefits they pay, the supply of affordable housing, the quality of our schools and the power we have over our lives.

The novelist Thomas Pynchon once wrote, "If they can get you to ask the wrong questions, they don't have to worry about the answers." So, for our film series, we began to pose new questions. Rather than simply ask, "How can we promote healthy behaviors?" we also asked, "How can we target dangerous conditions and reorganize land use and transportation policies to ensure healthy spaces and places?" Rather than just asking, "How can individuals protect themselves against health threats?" what about also asking, "How can community organizing and alliance building drive policies that protect the public good?" Rather than ask, "What populations are vulnerable?" what about also asking, "What causes the unequal distribution of health-promoting and health-harming conditions in the first place?"

3. Make Health Equity an "Us" Issue

We also wanted to make clear that health equity is a problem for all, and provides an opportunity to build cross-racial and cross-sectoral alliances. Following the conventional "right choices" frame, much of the public—especially middle-class White people—think of health gaps (when they think of them at all) as pertaining to "them" ("*those* people"): the poor and people of color.

But the wealth-health gradient suggests that it's not just that the rich are healthy and the poor are sick, but that the health of the great majority of Americans, perhaps 80 percent of the population, is threatened by the growing inequality between the rich and the rest of us and our degraded economic, social and built environments.

Second, there's a financial cost we all share: our sick-care system has hit the wall. We already spend more on health care per person than twice than the average rich country—more than 2.5 trillion dollars per year, one-sixth of our GDP. A healthier population would relieve the pressure on the medical system.

Third, unhealthy people are not productive and harm our competitiveness. According to a 2007 study by the Santa Monica-based Milken Institute, business is losing more than 1.2 trillion dollars a year and growing in lost productivity due to chronic illness.

Still, many believe that, at its core, the "us versus them" issue is about race—or, more precisely, *racism*. Our research suggested that unequal racial outcomes in particular were rationalized as the consequences of deficiencies in the culture, habits or even genes of the subordinated group. To make inroads, we felt it was particularly important that we move beyond racism as personal prejudice and render visible how opportunity structures operate to disproportionately channel power, status and wealth to White people.

4. Americans' Health is America's Choice

Since most Americans believe there's little that society or government can or should do to change health outcomes, we needed to make clear that our health inequities are not set in stone. They are not natural, nor are they inevitable. On the contrary, population health is a product of decisions we *have made*—not just as individuals but as a body politic—and *can make differently*. We've changed them before, and we can change them again.

We decided to raise this issue two ways:

A) Use history to demonstrate how population health tracks social changes and policy. Both racial and class health gaps narrowed in the wake of civil-rights victories and the war on poverty yet began widening again beginning in the early 1980s. This trend paralleled the growing inequality since the Reagan administration kicked off a three-decades-long project of cutting back social programs, giving tax cuts to the rich, and, most of all, deregulating our way into an unbridled free market and a degree of corporate power not seen since the Gilded Age.

One result is that we've fallen to 29th in both life expectancy and infant mortality. Similarly, many historians argue that the 30-year increase in life expectancy during the 20th century was driven not primarily by medical advances but rather by social changes that enabled productivity increases to be shared by ever-larger segments of the American population: the eight-hour work day, sanitation and housing codes, the right to collective bargaining, social security, banking and business regulation, a progressive income tax, the civil-rights and environmental movements, the war on poverty, Medicaid and Medicare. People lived longer because they lived *better*.

B) Appeal to national pride. Why don't we, the world's richest and most powerful nation, have the world's best health outcomes? What do the other rich nations have that we don't? Do they have better genes?

There *are*, though, arenas in which we are number one:

- *The greatest wealth inequality*
- *The highest poverty rate*
- *The highest child-poverty rate*
- *The smallest middle class*
- *The least social spending (as a percent of GDP)*
- *The highest incarceration rate (1/4 of the world's prisoners)*
- *The lowest voter-participation rate*

It's by now fairly common knowledge that the United States is the only rich country not to guarantee universal health care. Not so well-known is that it's also the only rich country not to guarantee, by law:

- *Paid vacations*
- *Paid sick leave*
- *Universal preschool*
- *Paid parental leave*

And if we lose our job, let alone our *home*, we're on our own. Sink or swim. These uncertainties and insecurities create chaos in people's lives, and chaos triggers the body's stress response, which, over the long term, wears out our organs prematurely. It's one reason that poor smokers are more likely to get sick than rich smokers. We felt that examples like this would help draw the connection between health and social policies.

5. A New Rx for Health: Social Policy Is Health Policy

What kind of programs can make a difference? What policies constitute a health-equity agenda? It's not enough to talk in the theoretical and abstract; we needed to define and promote concrete initiatives that can improve health equity, gain political traction and energize people. High-profile national-health-equity efforts have been launched in other countries. The social democracies of Europe make social investments that lessen inequality and also make access to many health promoters more universally available, independent of an individual's household resources. Drawing attention to domestic health-equity initiatives that held promise and communicated a sense of possibility proved to be our most difficult challenge.

6. Appeal to Common Sense

Finally, we felt it imperative to keep things simple. The logic and evidence are ample; investing in health equity makes good moral sense and good fiscal sense. In fact, it's *common* sense. We needed to make the arguments clearly, simply and concisely: investing in creating the conditions for health today is not a cost; it brings a return on investment in the form of a healthier, more prosperous and more equitable society tomorrow with less money spent on medical care, higher productivity and a healthier old age.

The Broadcast and the Campaign

This is not to say we were clear about all these issues from the beginning; they emerged as we zigzagged forward with planning and production. But finally, in late winter 2008, we found ourselves racing to complete our sound mix and launch our website and companion tools as the broadcast date loomed.

Unnatural Causes was first broadcast on PBS over four weeks beginning in March 2008 and ran in 98 of the top 100 markets. The series was hailed by the media as "riveting." On the *Today Show*, Matt Lauer called it "disturbing [and] startling," adding, "Hopefully, it will get a lot of people asking serious questions." *Newsweek* pointed out that the series "offers plenty of background... but the film's power comes not from experts or statistics but stories of real people."

McKinney & Associates used their understanding of the press to generate coverage that focused on the themes of the series. They sent out hundreds of screeners and press kits with backgrounders and briefs and targeted specific journalists for individual pitches and interviews. Their efforts paid off. *USA Today* wrote that the film "Explores why your bank account, race and zip code are more powerful predictors of healthiness than your medical coverage, habits and genes." The *Seattle Times* said, "Inequality is killing us. Behavior, diet and environment aren't always the answer. The stress of living in a win-or-lose society is." The *Los Angeles Times* tied health inequities to "the fetishistic worship of the so-called free market that increases the distance between the poor and the tax-averse rich ... only political will can provide a remedy." The longer-form radio interviews that McKinney booked for us also provided an opportunity to explore the roots of health inequities and their solutions in greater depth.

While the press hailed *Unnatural Causes* as a fresh and invaluable contribution to the national dialogue over health, the series won numerous honors, including an Alfred I. du Pont-Columbia Award and the Best Film/Radio/TV program of 2009 by the Academy of Sciences, Institute of Medicine, which brought it an even wider audience and enhanced credibility. But we wanted to go further; there is a difference between watching a film and *using* a film. During production, we had begun building outreach partnerships with numerous health and community organizations. They ranged from the Centers for Disease Control to the National Association of County and City Health Officials to advocacy groups like Black Women's Agenda and the California Pan-Ethnic Health Network, to the YMCA and the SEIU. It was these organizations that would breathe life into *Unnatural Causes* by integrating it into their work. We developed tool kits, action and discussion guides, backgrounders and other tools to help them. We and our advisors screened the series and led workshops at their conventions and annual meetings.

Eventually, more than 412 official partners and countless others convened more than 25,000 events built around *Unnatural Causes* in its first 18 months of release. They prompted new questions, sparked new conversations and organized new alliances between people who need to be involved in the effort to make us healthier: doctors, school boards, labor unions, city planners, racial justice advocates, churches, businesses and community-based organizations. More than 5,000 organizations are now integrating the series into their work. The *Unnatural Causes* e-newsletter provides educators and advocates regular news about best practices and updates of outreach tools and events and has a circulation of 21,000.

The Way Forward

When we began work with McKinney & Associates on *Unnatural Causes*, there was but one popular book and one major magazine article exploring the roots of our health gaps. Today, while health equity is far from a household word, the situation has changed considerably. Newspaper and magazine articles and radio reports, legislative and congressional testimony, city and county commissions, community forums and policy initiatives addressing health inequities are regular occurrences. And while these changes can't all be attributed to *Unnatural Causes*, the organizations involved all use *Unnatural Causes*.

Yet, *Unnatural Causes* is but one media project, and huge health-equity-communications challenges remain. For all the progress of the past few years, public opinion has yet to break free of the individual, biomedical model. Moving forward, should communications training and capacity-building be provided to health-equity organizations? Or should communications professionals be trained in health equity and then be brought together in a distinct communications entity that is somehow held accountable to the field? The answer, of course, is *both*. Health-equity groups must improve their communications capacity considerably, and they need the funds and training to do so. Communications should not be seen as an add-on but as a core organizational function.

It's probably too much to expect already overworked and hard-pressed health-equity organizations to take on yet another function (communications) and to do so with the expertise, élan, timeliness and creativity needed to make a significant impact on public opinion. On the other side, bankers and corporations view communications as vital and strategic to maintaining their power and influence. For decades, they have poured tens, probably *hundreds* of millions of dollars into building their communication capacities as individual companies through their trade associations, their lobbyists and their "think tanks." Their efforts need to be countered by an equally professional communications strategy—even if not as well financed.

Health equity is not rocket science, but it does demand that we reframe the way we look at health, expanding the lens so that it throws light on the role of our social and economic environments. It's like the story of the drunk crawling on his knees looking for his keys one night under the streetlight: A bystander watched him searching and finally spoke up, asking him, "What are you doing?"

> **Drunk:** "Looking for my keys."

> **Bystander:** "But you've looked and looked in that one area; they're obviously not there. Why do you keep on looking there?"

> **Drunk:** "That's where the light is."

With McKinney & Associates, we're beginning to broaden the light.

Afterword

GWEN MCKINNEY

There was no manual on how to do this thing called *public relations with a conscience*. In fact, the process of creating and building our organization was much like a toddler learning to walk. First steps are faltering. Then the sheer force of gravity and uncertainty lands you on your knees or butt – depending on how you tumble. You crawl, just enough to find an anchor to stand up again. The next fall is not so shattering and there are new methods quickly learned to remain upright. Soon, with both instinct and new confidence, one foot strides surely in front of the other and the process becomes connected to moving. Those small steps carry you to deliberate and destined places. Even as a grown up, there are times when you trip and fall; there are still barriers to be scaled and cleared. But the sure-footedness established in those early days sealed the certainty in the steps forward.

The journey is underway! You can run the marathon.

It is important to remember where we all began. Rarely, if ever, do we walk (or run) alone. In this kind of experiment of helping people and causes amplify their voice, companion travel is essential. From baby steps to leaps of faith, the commitment to justice has become a long distance race.

When the firm started in 1990, we plied our trade with an IBM Selectric II typewriter and a clunky Kaypro computer. Today, our associates are empowered with Smart Phones and Twitter feeds, moving at the speed of a click instantaneously able to reach across oceans. Little did we know way back when that the long and relentless hours of planning and pitching would be transformed into a world of 24/7 news cycle, shrinking elite media and an army of citizen journalists commanding their space in the Blogosphere. The business competitors back in the early 90s were virtually all white, male and mostly centrist. Few communications firms boasted a commitment to social justice as their market niche. And even fewer dared to dive in with nothing more than sweat equity and undaunted faith that doing the right thing would clear a path to a sound business model.

Little did we know... that the long and relentless hours of planning and pitching would be transformed into a world of 24/7 news cycle, shrinking elite media and an army of citizen journalists commanding their space in the Blogosphere.

With no crystal ball to look forward, the rearview assessment is illuminating. Other than vision in your mind's eye, that's all we have to navigate the future. No one told us that the marathon race would be unpredictable, damning and replete with unimaginable rewards and victories. And it was better that we didn't know. Hence, we keep trotting and moving, certain that the finish line is over the next big hill.

Truthfully, without our cohorts and clients there would be no race. We'd have no reason to be. The people who allowed the firm to be their collaborators are collectively and individually what defines McKinney – first as McKinney & McDowell, now as McKinney & Associates. Each campaign became another stroke of evidence that what we started is important and enduring.

When McKinney & Associates marked its 20th Anniversary in 2010, we wanted to celebrate with more than a party. Somehow, we needed to create a more permanent record of our work. Through the years, with our unique brand of public relations, didn't we write the book?

So there you have it. Our book, *Voice Matters: An Anthology of Public Relations with a Conscience.*

Part essay. Part memoir. Part how to. Part why do.

This collection is a glimpse back and forward, projecting a kaleidoscope of the people, partners and reasons that we exist. Voice is singular in our title, But in application it is myriad sounds and infinite tones of the many known and uncounted people who make our work matter. Each essay speaks for itself. But like all worthy voices, they resonate beyond the individual stories. Confined to word limits, more experiences are left out than included. But all that you read weave threads in a fabric that is our colorful, dynamic and still unfolding cloth.

As the essays came in, at times I was embarrassed by what seemed too much focus on me. *This is not about me.* Then I hear my own voice, counseling clients again and again, "You are a tangible form of what you profess and embody. Your presence is not personal; it's part of the message. The brand." So I accept my own advice, get over the discomfort of a referential spotlight, and embrace the pride to *represent* in the same bound pages with our *Voice Matters* contributors. They etch the indelible sum total of our many parts and positions.

Bob Herbert was preparing to leave the *New York Times* after 18 triumphant years when I asked him to provide the foreword. During much of his career, he and I had been in constant contact – we've commiserated, confided and conspired to expose true stories that might not otherwise have been told. It seemed most appropriate that the theme of his final column — a call to arms issued months before the 99 Percenters launched the Occupy Movement— would inform our opening salvo. Diane McKinney-Whetstone, among the very few souls (three other sisters clamor in the background) who knew me from day one, provides a personal peek into my world. It is as unpredictable and far-flung as the stories that follow her witty, sisterly introduction. Leila McDowell, who shares a vision birthed in the humble surroundings of the St.

Augustine Church basement, is still daring to transform the impossible into what must be.

That kind of spirit helped define our connection with people like Richard Montgomery, whose magic eye helps turn a thousand words into a powerful picture; Candice Francis, whose resolute definition of worth is true and self-affirming; Diann Rust-Tierney, whose commitment to save lives and convey the humanity of those condemned to Death Row tells our nation why we should do better; Jackie Jeter, a workers' leader, reminds us why heroes who toil for a living are often the most noble; Karen Narasaki, whose Pan-Asian experiment extols why diversity matters; Larry Adelman, whose imagination to create *Unnatural Causes* and willingness to let me come along for the ride further refined our firm's niche in today's crucial battle for health equity. New arrivals to our public relations fold include Michele Brown, offering a personal testimonial. We also salute the brilliant advocate Michelle Alexander, working to make the unjust walls of over-incarceration come tumbling down, and Susan Burton, the human face of that story, who inspires and shows most poignantly that though our individual efforts alone may seem slight, together with our allies we become mighty and heroic. Bibliophile and restaurateur Andy Shallal shares ingredients for a successful blend of culture, art and food, reaffirming that good business and good politics are not mutually exclusive.

The people who allowed the firm to be their collaborators are collectively and individually what defines McKinney...Each campaign became another stroke of evidence that what we started is important and enduring.

This conclusion is also an acknowledgment to the collaborators who have no byline here: James Johnson, who helped make our first clunky Kaypro computer work in the basement office and then continued to supply IT support at work as our technology advanced into the Internet age, and at home as my spouse; Elaine Jones, former head of the NAACP Legal Defense Fund, our longest sustained client from 1992 until 2007. Because Elaine with her magnetic wisdom believed in a start-up run by two African American women, others also took the risk; the civil rights advocacy community that was the vineyard where we labored for more than a decade with warriors like Mary Frances Berry, Bill Fletcher, Wade Henderson, Barbara Arnwine, and Karen Lawson to name only a few; Linda Wright Moore, senior communications officer with the Robert Wood Johnson Foundation, who understands that the voice of philanthropy without precision and empowerment might only be a paltry excuse for charity. Today she continues to cast her vote of confidence in our partnership. And to the exquisite scholar and literary activist E. Ethelbert Miller, more than an epilogue, thanks for the melodic bookends.

Finally, to our team that believes voice *is* what matters even when they are the invisible vessel that carries it. For Elaine Elinson, whose initials also stand for "Excellent Editor(!)"; Shawntay Warren, diligent first editorial coordinator; and to the other able hands on deck including Llenda Jackson-Leslie, Tamara Braunstein, Monique Brackett, Donna Lewis-Johnson, Pam Taylor, Shannon Mouton, Ryan Duncan, Nicole Hayes, Vincent Hughes, Phyllis Wilder and Danielle LeFlore. Thank you all for demonstrating that there is no "*I*" in TEAM. Through your collective spirit, you assert that the four letter word is blessedly a plural noun.

We end here. It is the beginning of a new chapter. As you close this book, our greatest wish is that we open the possibilities for more voices to matter and to ring loud and clear.

Fix Something That is Broken

E. ETHELBERT MILLER

(for Me-K)

When you rise
fix something that is broken.

It will make a difference
between yesterday and today.

Repair your heart
before you love.

Touch another person
with hands that whisper
(or kiss).

McKinney & Associates Highlights

20 YEARS OF PUBLIC RELATIONS WITH A CONSCIENCE: THEN, NOW, NEXT

October 1990

"Women at Work" shingle hangs in basement office in the St. Augustine Ecumenical Center; McKinney & McDowell Associates, aka Mc & Mc, is born as the first African American and female-owned PR firm in the nation's capital that expressly promotes social-justice advocacy.

1991

Metropolitan Washington Council AFL-CIO awards annual first retainer, making a significant investment in the fledgling firm to help amplify the voice of public-service workers. Mc & Mc moves from church basement to the lower-lobby space of Wider Opportunities for Women at 1325 G St., NW. Mc & Mc orchestrates communications campaign for the First National People of Color Leadership Summit on the Environment, signaling the beginning of the environmental-justice movement. For his second visit to the United States, South African president Nelson Mandela engages former anti-apartheid campaigners Mc & Mc to arrange a NewsMakers Luncheon at the National Press Club.

1992

National Organization for Women retains Mc & Mc to support the largest women's- and reproductive-rights gathering held to date, the March for Women's Lives on Capitol Hill.

1993

NAACP Legal Defense Fund's (LDF) newly appointed president, Elaine R. Jones, taps Mc & Mc as its Agency of Record (AOR); the nation's preeminent civil rights law firm remains the firm's longest retained client (1992–2006), and the partnership would solidify its brand as a racial justice communications expert.

1994

Both McKinney and McDowell join President Jéan Bertrand Aristide on his return to Haiti, after serving as his government's AOR during his exile in the United States (1992–1994).

1996

Alarmed over the treatment of women in US prisons and the victims of stun technology, Amnesty International (AI) USA chapter retains Mc & Mc to envision and execute *Human Rights—Not Just A Foreign Affair*, a campaign that enlisted Muhammad Ali and his daughter Laila and helped establish AI's US-focused program.

1997

Mc & Mc supports LDF in a three-year public-education campaign for Hampton University student Kemba Smith, wrongfully jailed for drug trafficking and granted clemency in 2000 by President Clinton, bringing international attention to unjust drug-sentencing laws.

1998

Mc & Mc tips award-winning *New York Times* columnist Bob Herbert, spurring other national media coverage for Lacresha Murray—wrongfully sentenced at age 11 to 25 years in an Austin, TX, prison but, under the glare of national attention, ultimately cleared by the Texas Supreme Court.

2000

Death row inmate Gary Graham is executed by the state of Texas after an unprecedented media campaign supported by McKinney focused on his innocence and gained international attention that helped move the national debate on the death penalty. McKinney would later receive an award from the National Coalition to Abolish the Death Penalty for the firm's support of the movement.

2001

Mc & Mc joins US Commission on Civil Rights in publicizing hearings and releasing a groundbreaking report on Florida's role in the 2000 presidential election that documented election irregularities and black voter disenfranchisement.

2002

McKinney & McDowell becomes McKinney & Associates, aka McKPR. A changed name, but the passion and mission remain the same: "public relations with a conscience."

2003

The Murder of Emmett Till by acclaimed filmmaker Stanley Nelson airs on PBS with the support of McKPR, engaged by the network and the filmmaker to launch a national media campaign that helped to reopen the investigation into the horrific murder that ignited the 20th-century civil-rights movement. The film wins an Emmy and other acclaimed recognition.

2004

McKPR envisions and manages communications activities marking the 50th anniversary of the historic *Brown v. Board of Education* ruling with national commemorations, reports, public advocacy and the PBS documentary by Stanley Nelson's Firelight Media—*Beyond Brown: Pursuing the Promise.*

2006

A partnership with LDF and the Lawyers' Committee in the run-up to New Orleans municipal elections gains partnership of McKPR, which conceives and manages a multitiered media campaign upholding voting rights for displaced Hurricane Katrina survivors.

2007

Foreshadowing the national health-care debate, McKPR manages communications for California Newsreel's acclaimed four-part PBS documentary series *Unnatural Causes: Is Inequality Making Us Sick?*—the most definitive television review on health equity.

McKPR leads communications effort of the Leadership Conference on Civil Rights coalition that culminates in reauthorization of the landmark Voting Rights Act, extending minority-voter protection for 25 years.

2008

McKPR emerges from a competitive bidding process as the managing firm among five communications agencies selected by the Robert Wood Johnson Foundation's Human Capital Portfolio to assist in strategic management and grantee support for the nation's largest health philanthropy.

2009

Reeling from deep state-budget cuts, the California Department of Public Health's Maternal, Child & Adolescent Health Program, in partnership with University of California, San Francisco's Center on Social Disparities in Health, engages McKPR to assist in envisioning a federally funded, public-education campaign supporting infant-health centers and Black women's health across the state.

McKinney & Associates crafts high-touch, high-tech communications strategies empowering clients and partners to leverage traditional earned-media outreach, grassroots advocacy and Web 2.0 technologies to amplify and spread their messages.

2010

Reflecting on 20 years of advocacy, support and service to progressive communications, McKPR marks the anniversary with recommitment to grow, thrive and respond to the challenges and opportunities of the new decade. Combining traditional earned-media and grassroots outreach with social networking, McKinney & Associates launches campaign for CNN Top 10 Hero of 2010 Susan Burton. McKinney team designs and manages multipronged, year-long communications campaign for award-winning RWJF demonstration, *Jobs to Careers*. The campaign showcased the nearly seven million frontline health-care workers who touch more lives than all other health-care professionals combined. In response to the nation's changing demographics, McKinney designed and implemented "IMAGINE Tomorrow...*The Future Begins Today*" to assist RWJF with generating a diverse applicant pool of health-care professionals who represent the array of cultural, socioeconomic and geographic backgrounds mirrored in the rich and changing tapestry of America.

Authors' Bios

Larry Adelman

Larry Adelman is co-director and head of production for California Newsreel, the country's oldest non-profit, documentary-film-production-and-distribution center. Adelman is the creator and executive producer of the award-winning documentary *Unnatural Causes: Is Inequality Making Us Sick?* and the pioneering PBS series *RACE—The Power of an Illusion.* He has appeared nationally, including the *Washington Post,* the *Nation,* the *San Francisco Chronicle,* the *Today Show* and *All Things*  *Considered.* He is currently developing *American Birthright,* a multimedia initiative that aims to reframe the way Americans think about early child health and development.

Michelle Alexander

Michelle Alexander is a longtime civil-rights advocate and litigator. She currently holds a joint appointment at the Kirwan Institute for the Study of Race and Ethnicity and the Moritz College of Law at Ohio State University. Alexander has served as director of the ACLU of Northern California's Racial Justice Project and directed the Civil Rights Clinic at Stanford Law School. She has written for the *New York Times, Sojourners* and the *Huffington Post* and has appeared as a commentator  on CNN, MSNBC and NPR. *The New Jim Crow: Mass Incarceration in the Age of Colorblindness* is her first book.

Tamara Braunstein

Tamara Braunstein, formerly a Junior Account Associate with McKinney, assisted the team with digital media and project support. A Seattle, Wash., native, she has called the East Coast "home" for the past six years. Prior to joining McKinney & Associates, Tamara worked as a communications contractor for the Institute for Policy Studies. She holds a M.A. in Journalism and Public Affairs from American University, and a B.A. in Spanish from the University of Pittsburgh. She was one of five in the Class of 2009 to receive the four-year Helen S. Faison scholarship award.

Michele Brown

Michele Reneé Brown is the founder of WordPlay Consulting, a boutique consulting firm based in Oakland, California, specializing in strategic communications, fund development and event management. As a senior advisor to national leaders in politics and civic life, Brown has made a name for herself as a program innovator, a successful grant writer and an effective communicator. She is a graduate of the George Washington University with a degree in International Affairs/Economics. She has worked in democratic politics since Jesse Jackson's presidential bid and served in both Clinton administrations.

Susan Burton

Susan Burton is the founder and director of A New Way of Life Reentry Project in Los Angeles, a program that has created a bridge for more than 600 formerly incarcerated women to sobriety, redemption, economic opportunity and political enfranchisement. In 2010, Burton was selected as one of CNN's Ten 10 Heroes and received honors from the Harvard University Center for Public Leadership and the Los Angeles Women of the NAACP.

She serves on the board of the Los Angeles Sober Living Network, which provides housing for thousands of homeless individuals in the city.

Candice Francis

Candice Francis is a gifted communicator with expertise in many communications disciplines. Her consulting practice, Consummate Communications, provides services for public-relations firms in Washington DC and northern California, supporting health-equity and social-justice endeavors. Francis writes and edits a wide range of communication tools and is a writing coach for individual projects, including personal memoirs. A familiar figure in northern-California media, Francis worked as a producer at KRON-BAY TV, KQED-FM and KQED-TV. She has also taught writing, critical thinking, public speaking and parenting communications at UC Berkeley and Peralta and Contra Costa community colleges.

Bob Herbert

Bob Herbert is an award-winning columnist who wrote about politics, urban affairs and social trends for the *New York Times* for nearly two decades. Previously, Herbert was a national correspondent for NBC and reported regularly on *Today* and *NBC Nightly News*. His career began in 1970 as a reporter at the *Star-Ledger* in Newark, New Jersey. Herbert has won awards from the American Society of Newspaper Editors and the Shorenstein Center at Harvard University and has also won the Ridenhour Courage Prize for the "fearless articulation of unpopular truths." He is the author of *Promises Betrayed: Waking Up from the American Dream*.

Jackie Jeter

A passionate advocate for transit workers, Jackie Jeter has won praise and criticism for her stances on worker safety and management accountability in the wake of the tragic 2009 Metro Red Line crash, which claimed nine lives.

Jeter rose from the position of part-time bus operator to become the first woman president of Amalgamated Transit Union (ATU) Local 689 in 2007. ATU Local 689 represents more than 10,000 current and retired Metropolitan Washington transit workers and is the third largest ATU local in North America.

Leila McDowell

Leila McDowell is a communications and public-relations expert who has spent 20 years building the power and impact of progressive organizations. A cofounder and former vice president of McKinney & McDowell Associates, she is currently the NAACP's vice president for communications. McDowell is a former reporter with WPIX-TV in New York, CNN, NPR, AP Radio, Inner City Broadcasting and Radio One. Her clients have included Al Gore's Alliance for Climate Change; Amnesty International; the Rockefeller Foundation; TransAfrica; the United Food and Commercial Workers International Union and the governments of Jamaica, Namibia, Mozambique, Angola and Venezuela.

Gwen McKinney

Gwen McKinney is founder and president of McKinney & Associates, the first African American female-owned firm in the nation's capital promoting social justice communications. McKinney's career in communications began as a *Philadelphia Tribune* reporter. Later, she became a Washington correspondent covering Congress and national policy for several newspapers, and she has written for *Essence* and *Black Enterprise* magazines. Press secretary for Representative Eleanor Holmes Norton during her first bid to Congress, Gwen specializes in social-policy and social-justice communications strategy and serves as a trusted advisor to many of the nation's most influential civil-rights leaders.

Diane McKinney-Whetstone

Diane McKinney-Whetstone grew up in Philadelphia, the setting for her latest novel, *Trading Dreams at Midnight.* She is currently the author of five novels, including the best-selling *Tumbling,* and her work has also appeared in *Philadelphia Magazine, Essence,* the *Sunday Philadelphia Inquirer Magazine* and the anthologies *Bluelight Corner* and *Mending the World.* McKinney-Whetstone's numerous awards include the American Library Association (Black Caucus) Literary Award for Fiction, a Pennsylvania Council on the Arts grant and the Zora Neale Hurston Society Award. She currently teaches fiction writing at the University of Pennsylvania and lives in Philadelphia with her husband, Greg.

E. Ethelbert Miller

E. Ethelbert Miller is the board chair of the Institute for Policy Studies and the director of the African American Resource Center at Howard University.

His poetry has been translated into Spanish, Portuguese, German, Norwegian, Tamil and Arabic and he has written two memoirs, FATHERING WORDS: THE MAKING OF AN AFRICAN AMERICAN WRITER (2000) and THE 5TH INNING (2009).

Mr. Miller has taught at UNLV, American University, George Mason University, and Emory and Henry College, and was a core faculty member with the Bennington Writing Seminars. He was awarded an honorary degree of Doctor of Literature from Emory and Henry College. Mr. Miller is the former chair of the Humanities Council of Washington, D.C.

Richard Montgomery

Richard Montgomery is a creative-design director, film-maker and brand-marketing specialist. He currently directs McKinney & Associates' conceptual design and development. His work with McKinney has included design and layout of a report marking the 40th anniversary of the assassination of Dr. Martin Luther King, Jr., collateral materials for the nationwide showings of the Newsreel film *Unnatural Causes* and online materials for the *BeWellWomen* campaign, sponsored by the California Department of Public Health. Montgomery received his degree in architecture from Hampton University. His film *Wardrobe Malfunction* was named best short film at the 2005 Cleveland International Film Festival.

Karen Narasaki

Karen Narasaki is president and executive director of the Asian American Justice Center, one of the nation's premiere civil rights advocacy organizations advancing the human and civil rights of Asian Americans to build and promote a fair and equitable society for all.

Karen is a national authority on immigration and civil rights, serving as vice chairwoman of the Leadership Conference on Civil Rights and head of the Rights Working Group. She is a board member of Common Cause and the Lawyers Committee for Civil Rights, and Nielsen Media and Comcast/NBC Universal advisory councils. She has been selected three times as one of the "100 most powerful women in Washington" by *Washingtonian Magazine*.

Diann Rust-Tierney

Diann Rust-Tierney became the executive director of the National Coalition to Abolish the Death Penalty in 2004, directing programs to change public policy on the death penalty. Previously, Rust-Tierney served as the director of the American Civil Liberties Union Capital Punishment Project, as chief legislative counsel and as associate director of its Washington DC office. During her tenure at the ACLU, she was the lead advocate on capital punishment on Capitol Hill, coordinating a coalition of national organizations on the issue. Previously, Rust-Tierney engaged in litigation and public-policy advocacy at the National Women's Law Center.

Andy Shallal

Andy Shallal moved to the U.S. from Iraq when he was 11 years old. After graduating from high school, Andy got into medical school at Howard University in Washington, D.C., but soon decided that it was not for him. He soon realized that the restaurant business was something he really loved. After running several other restaurants and closing them, in 2005 he opened Busboys and Poets in Washington, D.C. Andy's mission for this restaurant was to have a gathering place for people of all different incomes, races, and identities to come together and exchange ideas about social and political issues.

Pamela Taylor

Pamela Taylor is a freelance writer and communications consultant specializing in campaign development for both industry and government. Committed to the use of social media and green technology on behalf of underserved groups, she has produced numerous communications tool kits, including *Jobs to Careers: Transforming the Front Lines of Health Care* and *Environmental Health Hazards in the Nation's Low-Income Housing Stock*. An award-winning journalist, Taylor is a graduate of the Newhouse School of Public Communications at Syracuse University in New York.